More for Less

Companion Books by Andrew Spanyi

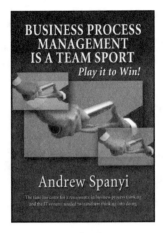

(Contributed Chapter)

Meghan-Kiffer Press
Tampa, Florida, USA
www.mkpress.com
Innovation at the Intersection of Business and Technology

More for Less

The Power of Process Management

Andrew Spanyi

Meghan-Kiffer Press
Tampa, Florida, USA, www.mkpress.com
Innovation at the Intersection of Business and Technology

Publisher's Cataloging-in-Publication Data
Spanyi, Andrew.
More for Less: The Power of Process Management / Andrew Spanyi, - 1st ed.
p. cm.
   Includes bibliographic entries, appendices, and index.
   ISBN-10: 0-929652-03-7   ISBN-13: 978-0-929652-03-0

   1. Management. 2. Leadership. 3. Technological innovation. 4. Executive ability.
   5. Organizational Effectiveness. 6. Strategic planning. 7. Organizational change.
   8. Reengineering (Management) 9. Process control: I. Spanyi, Andrew. II. Title

HD58.87.S6369 2006   Library of Congress Control Number: 2006921869
658.4'063–dc21   CIP

Published by Meghan-Kiffer Press
310 East Fern Street — Suite G
Tampa, FL 33604 USA

Any product mentioned in this book may be a trademark of its company.

Meghan-Kiffer books are available at special quantity discounts for
corporate education and training use. For more information, write
Special Sales, Meghan-Kiffer Press, Suite G, 310 East Fern Street,
Tampa, Florida 33604, or email mkpress@tampabay.rr.com

Meghan-Kiffer Press
Tampa, Florida, USA
Innovation at the Intersection of Business and Technology
Printed in the United States of America.   SAN 249-7980
MK Printing 10 9 8 7 6 5 4 3 2 1

Table of Contents

Preface

I first became interested in thinking about business in process terms in 1984. At the time I was the Director of Marketing and Product Development for Xerox Learning Systems in Canada, and Xerox had just launched the total quality program, Leadership Through Quality.

Thinking about business in a process context was not just a revelation for me at the time. It provided an answer to what had been a puzzling issue. In my role at Xerox Learning Systems (XLS), I managed the development of dozens of custom training programs. They were all developed with a keen attention to detail, and based on best practice learning methodology and design. Yet, some programs worked and some didn't. I didn't really know why. It wasn't until I began looking at the client's business in process terms that the answer became apparent. Whenever a program did not deliver the anticipated benefits, the problem was not a skill or knowledge deficit. Invariably, the problem was related to the underlying business process. Often, it wasn't simply about workflow; there was a direct link to a deficit in leadership mindset and behavior.

In 1991, as an independent consultant, I met Dr. Geary Rummler, and I then began to understand more fully the power of process thinking. During the past 14 years, I've participated in over 135 process improvement projects, either as a consultant, relationship manager, or managing partner affiliated with The Rummler-Brache Group, or as an independent practitioner.

There's no magic to process improvement and management. But it does require a management mindset and behavior that is different from the norm.

Management mindset and behavior are precisely what this book is about. I've observed that the nature of management thinking hasn't changed all that much in the past 14 years. There is still too much command and control behavior out in the marketplace, and the traditional, functional view of business is still dominant in spite of significant advances in both management theory and technology. This continues to have an adverse impact on sustaining customer focus.

This book provides guidance to those leaders who are dedicated to managing their organizations such that "more for less" is created for both customers and shareholders.

If anything, this is a "prequel" and not a sequel to my first book, *Business Process Management is a Team Sport: Play It to Win!*

The "team sport" book is a business novel, and it assumes a certain depth of understanding of the value of process thinking at the enterprise level. However, it may have required a level of sophistication that many leaders simply don't yet have.

I am deeply indebted to Alan Brache, Brad Power, Roger Tregear, and Steve Smith for their comments after reviewing an earlier draft of the manuscript. Dr. Tom Davenport's comments on a later draft were also very valuable. This book is far better because of their insights and constructive criticism.

I am grateful to all the participants in the Mindset Study. In particular, for the insights provided by Dave Burritt, Todd Coffee, Jim Conway, Chuck Laurenti, George Maszle, Ed Maggio, Peter McCormick, Risan Øystein, Timo Raikaslehto, and Michael Treacy. I am also deeply thankful for the comments made by a number of people on certain aspects of the manuscript including Sue Bushell, Bryan Frew, George Diehl, Tom Dwyer, Peter Fingar, Stephen Graham, Mark McGregor, Robert Pearce, Michael Rosemann, Dick Smith, Steven Stanton, Steve Towers, and Ken Vollmer.

This is not a technical book. It is designed for leaders – executives, senior managers, and those tasked with transforming their business into a more customer-centric, high performing organization. It emphasizes the central role of leadership attitude and aptitude in process management. It proposes that a customer-centric view of business in a process context represents an important additional dimension of management.

I hope you enjoy it.

Andrew Spanyi
Oakville, Ontario and Manchester, CT, *March 2006*

One

More For Less

There is only one boss. The customer. And he can fire everybody in the company from the chairman on down, simply by spending his money somewhere else.
—Sam Walton

What do your customers really want? More for less, of course! That can hardly come as a surprise to you. After all, whether you are a senior executive, a middle manager, or a front line worker, you're a customer yourself.

As a customer, what "more" do you want? More value, more service, more consistent, flawless delivery performance, more accuracy, and even more responsiveness? You bet. Chances are that increasingly, you want to pay "less" for this "more," don't you?

Your customers are no different, and that's a problem because unless you can provide your customers with "more for less," you can be assured they will find someone else who can, and sooner rather than later.

Are you fully prepared to provide your customers with what they have come to expect and will increasingly demand? Do you understand that this requires a fundamental shift in conventional wisdom? Do your leaders appreciate that this involves working collaboratively in a new way? Do they understand that this must involve not only the improvement of individual business processes, but also the application of process concepts and principles across the entire enterprise value chain?

These are not theoretical questions. Customer expectations aren't likely to cool down anytime soon.

In a 2004 survey, 85 percent of the 2,000 US senior executives and managers surveyed acknowledged their customers' expectations are higher than they were two years before.[1]

And it's not just human nature and the desire for progress that are driving these soaring customer expectations. The wired customer, able to access information from anywhere in the world in an instant, is an ever more sophisticated and demanding consumer. In today's real-time world, customers who receive a rapid response from one supplier expect it from all others. Companies that fail to deliver can expect to lose out big time.

Better-informed customers know their options. Having instant access to reliable data on alternative product offerings or services makes them ornery. Furthermore, wired consumers expect to be rewarded well for their loyalty.

Are firms rising to this challenge?

Hardly. In their book, *Simply Better,* Barwise and Meehan argue that far too many firms are simply paying lip service to the adage that "The customer is king." Indeed, as they point out, data on customer satisfaction (depicted in Figure 1.1) suggests there has been virtually no improvement in the American Customer Satisfaction Index over the period 1994 through 2003.[2]

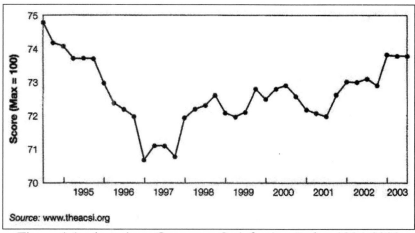

Figure 1.1. American Customer Satisfaction Index 1994-2003

In some sectors, the quality of service to customers may actually have declined. The Operations Council reported in a 2002 study,

Financial institution customers across the globe indicate that service is poor despite significant investments by
the industry to improve satisfaction and retain customers.
Meeting customer needs is no easy task in an environment
where distribution channels have exploded, product demand has become sophisticated, and customers regularly
switch relationships or split business among several providers.[3]

The reality, as highlighted by these sobering results, is that the
rise in customer expectations is plainly outstripping the ability of
firms to deliver on customer requirements. The sheer pace of
change is part of the problem. It took 15 years for 25 percent of
households to adopt personal computers after they first became
commodities a couple of decades ago. It took just 13 years to
achieve the same saturation ownership of cell phones, but less than
7 years for 25 per cent of households to hook up to Internet. Because the World Wide Web eliminates barriers of time and distance,
it accelerates the adoption of other new technologies. Just consider
how long it took different technologies to reach 10 million customers: 20 years for radio, 10 years for TV, 2.3 years for Netscape, and
1 year for Napster. An even more startling statistic is that the Web
has connected as many people in just 5 years as the phone company
did in an entire century, and now Internet traffic is reported to be
quadrupling annually.[4]

Yet with the exception of a handful of companies, firms simply
haven't come to grips with the full implications of increased customer power, and so have failed to modify their business practices
to deliver what customers want most: more for less.

What they have missed is that basic service delivery isn't
enough to differentiate an organization in today's market environment. Propelling a company beyond simple customer satisfaction to
the type of relationships that can drive business growth demands a
more profound understanding of the services customers value, as
well as employees who are empowered and motivated to interact
with those customers the way the customers want.

Companies have not fully grasped that when customers say

they want "more for less," what they really mean is

More	Less
▪ More value	▪ Less hassle
▪ More responsiveness	▪ Less sales pressure
▪ More of a say	▪ Less time
▪ More attentiveness	▪ Less talk about policy
▪ More trustworthiness	▪ Less expense
▪ More flexibility	▪ Less bureaucracy

Table 1.1. More for Less: the Customer Perspective

Perhaps it's due to a culture of navel-gazing that many firms still think they can manage their business by focusing principally on internal factors. They make little attempt to collaboratively manage the end-to-end flow of work that crosses the traditional organizational boundaries and creates value for customers.

Instead of focusing on providing customers with more for less, the predominant mental model in many traditional firms is "more with less," – more revenues, more earnings, and more cash flow – with less expense.

But revenues, earnings, and cash flow are *outcomes*. You can't manage outcomes. However, you certainly can and should manage the activities that create desired outcomes. Just ask any exemplary sales manager. He or she will tell you that you can't manage the top line – you can only manage the activities that produce the top line – leads, sales calls, proposals, and the conversion rate of leads-to-sales calls, sales calls-to-proposals, and proposals-to-revenue.

Oh yes – companies which subscribe to the "more with less" philosophy pay lip service to phrases like "customer delight," "moments of truth," and so on – but that isn't what guides their state of mind and actions.

You'd be amazed how few of these traditional companies even have a schematic that defines the flow of large, cross-functional activities that create value for customers. The only schematic that such organizations have of the enterprise is an organization chart –

and if that is the only schematic they have, and then position titles and business structures, which mean nothing to their customers, this will understandably dominate management thinking.

When you deal with these companies, you are likely to hear "I'm sorry, but that's not my department" and "I'm sorry, that's our policy." What these companies want is more of the top line and more of the bottom line, with less employees and resources. Imagine how their employees feel about that!

Employees are not much happier with the "more with less" philosophy than customers. Employees often find themselves working more and more and achieving less and less. They also see merit in the philosophy of "more for less." Their perspective bears a resemblance to the customers they serve, yet it is slightly different.

More	Less
▪ More leadership ▪ More clarity on the company's purpose ▪ More collaboration ▪ More time to innovate ▪ More recognition	▪ Less pressure ▪ Less bureaucracy ▪ Less emails, meetings ▪ Less of a need for individual "heroics" ▪ Less talk (more action)

Table 1.2. More for Less: the Employee Perspective

Why is it that companies struggle in shifting management practices from the "more with less" paradigm to giving customers more for less? There are several underlying reasons:

▪ **Myopic measurement practices.** Traditional financial measures of revenue, expenses, earnings, and cash flow dominate. The metrics that really matter to customers – on time receipt of product or service (complete and defect free), an accurate and user-friendly invoice, rapid and courteous responsiveness – often don't make it to the front page of the executive dashboard or scorecard. Even when they are monitored, the next level of diagnostic measurements is usually missing and the infrastructure for corrective action is either lacking or flawed. The impact of these myopic measurement practices is compounded by misaligned recognition and reward systems. Recognition and reward systems are not aligned with providing customer with "more for less." Instead, recognition and reward systems are designed according to what is being measured, that being the traditional financial metrics.

- **No accountability.** Far too often, no one is accountable for the end-to-end flow of activities that truly matter to customers. Often, the end-to-end activity flows are neither concisely defined, nor understood in the same way. No one is tasked with the performance monitoring and continuous improvement of the entire flow of activities from receipt of order to delivery of the firm's product or service. No one is tasked with the stewardship of the end-to-end flow of activities from idea generation to successful commercialization of a new product or service. Instead, the common practice is to assign accountability solely according to business unit, departmental, or functional parameters.

- **Lack of focus.** In the absence of a compelling business model, combined with myopic measurement practices, most firms launch more concurrent projects than they can successfully execute. Valuable resources are deployed on overlapping and sometimes even redundant projects. This is particularly true of essential information technology resources, which in this day and age are invariably part of practically any improvement effort.

The root cause of myopic measurement, lack of accountability, and lack of focus is attitudinal. These factors are symptoms of thinking in piecemeal fashion and failing to view the organization systemically. As any coach of a major sports team will tell you, having the right attitude is just as essential to winning as is having the right skill sets or aptitude.

The development of the right attitude or mindset remains one of the major challenges in viewing the enterprise in terms of the broad, cross-functional activities that create value for customers. In many organizations, the traditional functional view of the enterprise remains the predominant perspective. In this paradigm, activities and success are perceived in terms of power and authority defined by the organization chart. This is largely due to the simple fact that most leaders have a strong functional bias, which has been nurtured by both their academic and business experience.

Accordingly, instead of focusing on a shared understanding and the deliberate improvement of the firm's large cross-functional processes, managers tend to view processes at a micro level as "procedures," which represents the bias of their traditional functional management view.

This traditional view promotes a set of values and beliefs that stand in the way of customer centricity, adaptability, and agility. It underpins an "inside-out" view of how the business works. It lends emphasis to the misguided perspective that we really know what our customers want – without actually asking them. It tends to reinforce a short-term focus on making money as opposed to gaining clarity on the firm's principal purpose. It promotes the constant search for the "silver bullet" that will kill the werewolves of the competition.

There are also certain skill deficits when it comes to having the aptitude to consciously and effectively manage the cross-functional activities involved in developing and delivering products or services to customers.

The principal skill set most frequently lacking is the means to develop an enterprise level view of the business in terms of the cross-functional activities that constitute the company's value chain and create value for customers. Such a viewpoint is an essential ingredient in shifting the leadership perspective from a traditional functional paradigm to more of a customer centric perspective. That is what the firm's leaders need in order to develop a shared understanding of the company's performance in terms of its value-chain, or capabilities or processes.

An enterprise level schematic establishes the basis for the organization to express its strategic direction in terms of needed improvements in its critical cross-functional flows of activity. It also enables the firm to translate and relate the firm's performance, based on factors such as timeliness and quality in providing customers with "more for less," into more tangible statistics such as earnings and cash flow, and thereby correlate an improvement of X% in perfect order delivery to statistics like "days of sales outstanding" (DSO) or asset intensity.

When it comes to teamwork, you may have noted that leaders have little practice in working together in a deliberate and collaborative way. Many executive teams are more like a group of talented individuals than a team. As Smith and Blakeslee emphasize in their book *Strategic Six Sigma,* many executives let their strong need to exert control, their unsuitability for "shirtsleeves" work, and their massive egos get in the way of working as a leadership team on improving the cross-functional business processes.[5]

In other words, in order to provide customers with "more for less," a firm must become more adept at managing the performance of the firm's large, cross-functional processes in a deliberate and collaborative way. This management practice has become known as "process management." It's not just about reengineering. It's not just about Six Sigma. Certainly tool sets such as reengineering and Six Sigma have some role to play, but process management is more about a business process orientation throughout the enterprise, and it calls for a dramatically different way of thinking and acting. In a nutshell, it requires that leaders have both the right attitude and aptitude to define, improve, and manage the company's value chain. This is as true in business as it ever was in sports.

Let's understand. Managing a firm's large cross-functional processes, while an enormous challenge, is but one piece of the puzzle, albeit an important piece.

Of course, at most firms, the principal objective is to perform for the firm's shareholders. That is what tends to dominate leaders' thinking.

The good news is that providing customers with "more for less" is totally consistent with providing returns to shareholders. Perhaps Ben Verwaayen, CEO, British Telecom, stated it most concisely during a BBC Working Lunch interview in 2004 when he said, "The performance of shareholders is best served if we perform for our customers." He then went on to say, "The fact is I think it is a matter of behavior and mindset."[6]

What executive behaviors and what leadership mindset are needed for firms to perform for both customers and shareholders? That is what this book is about.

It provides you with guidance on why leaders should undertake a sustained effort to understand, improve, and manage the flow of value adding activities that typically cross the firm's traditional organizational boundaries. It will clarify that what is needed, in part, is a conscious shift in conventional wisdom in terms of the core management practices in five critical areas – strategy, broad based engagement, leadership, growth, and mergers. It will also provide you with some insight on the principal mental model challenges to overcome in paying close attention to how the firm creates value for customers and shareholders in managing the flow of cross-functional work.

Let's consider the importance of mindset. Why is it that in spite of a long and rich history of process thinking in the business literature little attention has been given to the benefits of managing the firm's cross-functional activities as they relate to topics such as strategy, engagement, leadership, growth, innovation, and mergers? Why is it that in spite of the compelling logic that work gets done by means of business processes, most companies continue to cling to a traditional, functional view of the business?

There are at least three possible reasons. Leaders don't care. Leaders can't focus. Leaders don't know how.

The proposition that executives don't really care about operations was put forth by Dr. Michael Hammer in a recent *Harvard Business Review* article. Hammer proposed that the general business culture holds operations in low esteem. Instead, he said, making acquisitions, planning mergers, and selling divisions are what senior managers think is really important. That's what gets a CEO's picture in the paper. Operations simply aren't glamorous, or sexy. What's more, operations are out of sight and out of mind. Senior executives are busy working on strategic planning, budgeting, capital allocation, and other so-called macro issues.[7] Let the "little people" worry about operations.

Then there's the argument that executives are aware of the importance of providing customers with value, but there's just too much going on to focus on improving operational performance. After all, as Dr. Tom Davenport points out, corporate attention is a zero sum game.[8] In the typical corporation there is so much activity that it's may be a challenge to maintain sustained focus on how the firm is performing for customers. Most organizations have dozens of initiatives competing for executive attention. Focusing on process performance as simply an initiative would just be yet another initiative added to the list. There's more than a grain of truth to this.

Yet another view is that leaders simply don't know how. They have elected to take a very narrow view of process. They have chosen to interpret the definition of process in a very technical, mechanical way as a set of "procedures." This may be fine for one-time process improvement efforts, especially those with a cost reduction objective. Such efforts periodically even yield some benefits to customers. But they certainly fall short of what is needed for the ongoing improvement and management of a company's business processes in any disciplined way. Perhaps that's why, even though business is arguably the most demanding of team sports, leadership teams don't practice. That is, they don't practice or role-play how the organization performs for customers. At the enterprise level, they don't understand how the flow of value added activity creates value for customers. If they knew how, wouldn't they measure what's important to customers in a disciplined way? Wouldn't they assign accountability for the performance of the company's large business processes, instead of opting to assign accountability purely in terms of functional or business unit lines? Wouldn't they want to deploy enabling technology with a view on the degree of its impact on performing for customers? Wouldn't they design recognition and reward systems with the intent of acknowledging the teams of people who do most to improve operational performance?

Of course, leaders would do all these things if they cared enough to invest the time and energy, were able to devote sufficient attention for sustainability, and knew how.

If the simple logic that "all work is done through business processes" doesn't work, then maybe the universal motivator of fear will serve to influence leadership mindset and behavior in just the right way. Or maybe common sense will prevail after all.

The triple threat of increasing customer power, commoditization, and globalization will strike fear in the hearts of leaders sooner or later. These three undeniable forces are not hype. The increasing power of the customer is not likely to fade away. In 2005, the use of high-speed connectivity in the US finally eclipsed the use of dial-up connectivity. Over 50 million consumers in the US alone now have access to a wide array of choices and instant information through broadband connectivity. This universal connectivity is what is driving business-to-business (B2B) interactions. Choice and information breed power for both business customers and consumers.

Similarly, the relentless march of commoditization is likely to continue apace. Offering a great product simply isn't enough anymore; any great product will surely be copied, duplicated, and ultimately commoditized. Only the most tightly interwoven product-service offerings have a chance to remain exempt from commoditization. Thinking about the business in the context of end-to-end workflow becomes an imperative when service delivery is combined with product attributes.

The impact of globalization, the growing interdependence between all people on this earth, is just beginning to be felt. Even white-collar knowledge workers, historically the source of competitive advantage for the Western economies, are increasingly under its grip.

"Only the paranoid survive," warns Intel's Andy Grove.[9] Under the combined forces of ever increasing customer power, commoditization, and globalization, we have been thrust into the midst of a strategic inflection point. Will common sense prevail, and will the needed shifts in executive mindset and behavior take place?

Only if there is a shift away from traditional, functional thinking will leaders undertake a sustained effort to understand, improve, and manage the firm's large cross-functional business processes.

Only then will they become not just aware, but also engaged in the need to reframe conventional wisdom as it relates to strategy, leadership, and growth. They will begin to focus on what is needed to answer the fundamental question: "Which of our key processes need to be improved, and by how much, in order to achieve our goals?"

Then leaders will begin to pay more attention to the problematic nature of the traditional functional mindset, and work on the collaborative behaviors needed to define, improve, and manage the performance of the firm's large cross-functional business processes to create value for customers.

They will then acknowledge that, although organization structure is important, what really counts is clear accountability for the improvement and management of the company's critical business processes, customer focused measures of performance, aligned recognition and reward systems, and broad collaboration across the formal organizational boundaries, with a focus on serving the needs of customers.

This type of thinking will also reframe the role of information technology (IT). Successful executives will come to appreciate the need to take more of a shared accountability for the deployment of IT, and deploy IT principally to enable the performance of their people in serving customers.

Instead of focusing slavishly on any one given improvement method, they will see that an integrated approach to improvement, where the focus is on strategic priorities and the intelligent use of a set of tools, can take organizations to a new plane of operational performance.

It's equally important to recognize what the philosophy of "more for less" and process thinking is not about:

- It's not about the conventional, linear mapping of processes. While mapping processes in a linear sense may have some role to play, it is the more comprehensive view of how work flows across traditional organization boundaries that creates more profound insight on performance. Thoughtful executives have already, or will soon, recognize that there is little value of linear thinking in a non-linear world.

- It's not about proposing that process thinking, in any form, is the end in itself. Instead, process orientation and tool sets are the means to create context for the company's value chain and get results for customers and shareholders.

- It's not simply about a form of abstraction, be it process models or anything else. While process models may have a useful role, it is a common understanding of the process view, accompanied by the right metrics, and a solid plan that have more to do with how organizations, especially the large, complex companies, need to change to get work done differently and better. In this context, process orientation becomes an additional and important dimension of management in leveraging organization capability.

- It's not really about technology. Technology, especially information technology, is available to all.[10] Even the most breakthrough information technology is replicated rapidly by fast followers. What counts is how you deploy it to gain a process advantage.

For many firms, the development of the necessary mindset and behaviors is going to be a long journey. To illustrate some of the opportunities and challenges, a number of interviews with frontline executives and managers, based on a recently conducted qualitative survey, went into the making of this book.[11] The basic premise for this qualitative survey, called the Mindset Study, was that a company creates value for customers and shareholders via the effectiveness and efficiency of activities or work which flows across traditional organization boundaries – often referred to as the firm's complex cross-functional business processes. Interviews were conducted with eighteen (18) respondents from businesses who were considered to have advanced levels of process orientation.[12]

The primary objective of this qualitative research was to gain some insight into the following:

- To what extent do leaders have a shared understanding of the

enterprise's business processes?
- Do business leaders have the right mindset for enabling process management?
- Are the right (customer-oriented) performance metrics in place?
- What process improvement methods are most in vogue?
- What are the major obstacles in deploying process management principles and practices?

The two primary insights derived from this qualitative research were thought provoking. (1) There is increasing interest and skill in improving a single cross-functional business process. (2) The traditional mindset of leaders continues to be one of the major obstacles in taking process management principles and practices to the next level where there is sustainable focus on the improvement and management of the firm's set of enterprise-level business processes.

The research set out to identify the set of leadership behaviors, based on both aptitude and attitude, which organizations need in order to deploy process management effectively. The hypothesis was that firms that have embraced business process management at the enterprise level would have:
- Developed an enterprise view of the business in process terms – a schematic or map, if you will;
- Appointed business process owners or stewards for some of the firm's large cross-functional business processes;
- Linked key performance metrics from a customer's point of view to key financial metrics, and monitored these metrics regularly at the leadership level.

The findings were revealing. Respondents were identified based on their stated interest in process improvement and management. Even among these corporations, who considered themselves to be more business process oriented than the average, only:
- Six of the 18 respondents – or 33 percent – reported having an enterprise view business process relationship map.
- Six of the 18 respondents – or 33 percent – reported having process owners – but upon further discussion only four re-

spondents confirmed that these owners were at the top team level.

- Six of the 18 respondents – or 33 percent – reported having customer touching metrics that were regularly monitored at the top team level. However, several additional respondents reported significant progress in this area at the local level.

Other indications of progress in improving and managing the firm's large cross-functional business processes included:

- The chief executive officer of a major office products firm was reported to "own" the "quote to cash" process personally and regularly monitor performance of this process;
- The corporate controller for a heavy equipment manufacturing company reported solid progress on the global process ownership of the CPI or continuous product improvement process and the global purchasing process.

Yet even those organizations that have made significant progress in elevating senior management attention to the enterprise business processes still see mindset and behavior challenges.

The results of this qualitative research, in combination with this author's insights from over a decade of consulting experience, speaking with other professionals at process management conferences and related events, served to crystallize two fundamental convictions.

First, leaders need to reframe their thinking with respect to the role of customer centricity and process thinking. This involves a fundamental shift in conventional wisdom as it relates to a broad range of management practices pertaining to strategy formulation and implementation, leadership, employee engagement, growth, and mergers. This attitudinal shift needs to precede the development of the requisite skill sets needed to perform for customers.

Second, the essential business principles and practices of process management need to be more broadly understood. Only then will organizations be well positioned to hone their skills in the following six critical areas of management practice that are shown in Table 1.3.

	What's Needed	What's Involved
1	An enterprise view or schematic and a plan on performing for customers	Measure what counts to customers Define the set of enterprise business processes Build a process management plan that bridges performance gaps such that goals will be met Build and deploy a communication plan on which processes need to be improved by how much for the firm to achieve its goals
2	Design enterprise business processes to deliver on its goals	Take action to improve the top priority processes Manage the set of enterprise business processes
3	Ensure that organization design enables enterprise business process execution	Make refinements to organization design, to align structure, roles, accountabilities, recognition, and reward systems
4	Deploy information technology based on the value added to business process performance	Invest in IT in accordance with the estimated improvement in process performance
5	Tightly link the enterprise performance measurement system to budgets and operating reviews	Include customer centric metrics in monthly operating reviews Express the impact of improving process performance in financial terms
6	Deploy an integrated improvement method to sustain focus	Invest in an integrated method of process improvement Continue to invest in training and reinforcing key messages

Table 1.3. Critical Areas of Management Practice

It's important to recognize that the framework represented by the above management practices involves nothing less than a new leadership mindset and a new set of leadership behaviors. This is especially true when it comes to measurement and governance. You will find that the themes of 1) measuring what matters to customers, and 2) establishing accountability for the improvement and management of the company's cross-functional business processes pervade the six management practices cited above.

The power of the process management perspective produces significant potential benefits. These include:

- Sustainable focus on what matters to customers
- The development of a performance oriented culture
- A framework for superb execution, where strategies are translated into action, results are measured, and the organization's capabilities are leveraged
- The means to break down internal fiefdoms or silos that stand in the way of performing for customers and shareholders

To bring further focus on these factors, several of the subsequent chapters includes specific guidance on how you can assess progress and a series of self-assessment questions.

References.

[1] Demanding Customers, *Darwin Magazine*, September 2004

[2] Barwise, Patrick and Sean Meehan, *Simply Better: Winning and Keeping Customers by Delivering What Matters Most*, Harvard Business School Press, 2004

[3] Engaging the Customer: Building Customer-Driven Operations, Operations Council, 2002.

[4] Harris, Jim, *Blindsided*, Capstone Publishing, 2002

[5] Smith, Dick and Jerry Blakeslee with Richard Koonce, *Strategic Six Sigma; Best Practices from the Executive Suite*, Wiley, 2002

[6] http://news.bbc.co.uk/2/hi/programmes/working_lunch/3739278.stm

[7] Hammer, Michael, 'Deep Change: How Operational Innovation can Transform Your Company', *Harvard Business Review*, April 2004

[8] Davenport, Thomas H., 'Attending to Processes', *BPTrends*, March 2004

[9] Grove, Andrew S., *Only the Paranoid Survive*, Currency, 1999.

[10] Carr, Nicholas G., *Does IT Matter? Information Technology and the Corrosion of Competitive Advantage*, Harvard Business School Press, 2004

[11] Conducted in the latter half of 2004 and early 2005.

[12] The findings were published as a process management research report by Babson College's Process Management Research Center

Two

The Power of Process: Shifting Conventional Wisdom

Observation, not old age, brings wisdom.
– Publilius Syrus

Providing customers with "more for less" demands a new way of thinking about business. It requires that customer centricity and value chain concepts be in the forefront of management thinking and acting. Much has been written on the merits of viewing business in terms of the key cross-functional activities that transcend traditional organizational boundaries, yet, to date the key principles and practices simply haven't broadly penetrated management behavior. What's needed is a subtle shift in conventional wisdom in relationship to deeply held views on strategy and execution, engagement, leadership, and other management practices as organizations seek to provide customers with "more for less."

The acceptance of the need for a shift in conventional wisdom is not new. Over a decade ago, Dr. Tom Davenport summarized some of the then widely held customer unfriendly views such as:

- We're smarter than our customers.
- We know what they really need.
- Our primary and overriding purpose is to make money, to produce near-term shareholder return.
- Our key audience is the financial market, especially the analysts.
- The primary way to influence corporate performance is through portfolio management and creative accounting.
- Managers are paid to make decisions. Workers are paid to do, not think.
- The job of senior managers is strategy, not operations.

- If it isn't broken, don't fix it.[1]

These customer unfriendly views are the product of traditional functional thinking. That's what stands in the way of companies performing for customers. Indeed, the traditional functional mindset of leaders remains the principle obstacle to the practice of process management at the enterprise level. Why is that? Part of the answer is that we have been conditioned by our education and our experience.

Most of us studied a particular academic discipline in college, be it marketing, finance, IT, or engineering. Then, for most of us, our first job was in the same functional area that we studied, be it marketing, finance, IT, or engineering. In most cases, career progression was based on demonstrating excellence in that same area of functional responsibility.

It is this type of background that leads to 'silo' behavior and 'turf protection.' So it should come as little surprise that many leaders view the world through a functional bias. Jim Conway, the former Chief Operating Officer of the Dana Farber Cancer Institute said, *"In health care – the org chart gets in the way of care delivery."*

And it's not just in health care. The organization chart does get in the way of flawless product or service delivery in a broad cross section of industries, largely due to the perception of the organization as a group of functional entities. You can call them silos. You can call them fiefdoms. Whatever the name, the products of traditional functional thinking include inefficiency, ineffectiveness, stifled creativity, insularity, and inconsistent follow-through.[2] A value chain based process perspective of business is one of the only options for tearing down the walls of these silos or fiefdoms.

While there is a long and rich history of process thinking in the business literature, in recent years the practical application of process thinking has had more to do with cost reduction than anything else. The relatively narrow view of process is due in part to the failure of leaders to understand why they should undertake a sustained effort to understand, improve, and manage the firm's large cross-functional business processes. So, instead of "more for less," the predominant practical theme has been "more with less."

"More with less" is a consequence of thinking about business in traditional terms. Proponents of "more with less" focus primarily on internal factors. Even though the rhetoric may be on providing customers with "more for less," the thrust of improvement activity is mainly on cost reduction. Sadly, this is true in many cases for both reengineering and Six Sigma efforts.

Only a handful of subject matter experts have written about the value of a systemic view of the enterprise within the extensive literature on reengineering, TQM, and Six Sigma. Accordingly, the concept of "process" has become synonymous with improvement versus ongoing management, in both reengineering and Six Sigma. Arguably, Dr. Michael Hammer's work represents the most influential writing on the topic of reengineering. While Hammer has written extensively on customer centric concepts such as being "easy to do business with" (ETDBW),[3] what remains in the forefront of many leaders' minds are his more radical views, as reflected in his landmark 1990 HBR article "Reengineering Work – Don't Automate, Obliterate."[4] The level of thinking about process might best be illustrated by the comments of Michael Treacy, a widely recognized expert on corporate strategy and business transformation, who, when asked his views on process management, replied that he had the following two major concerns. First, that it provides "an incomplete view," a comment, he said, that applies more to some processes than to others.

"If we are talking order to cash, then obviously the process view works fairly well because it's a fairly mechanical set of steps. But if one is talking about the process of sales, for example, you can, of course, create a mechanical view that results in sort of a sales pipeline view – if you will – on how sales take place. But, of course, it weeds out certain important elements of what really happens in the sales process, which is the building of trust between two individuals, how you create alliances in the client organization, and create alignment within the client organization, too, that has everyone agreeing – and that type of thing. Those are not well captured by a process model. So there are processes like sales or the product innovation process where the process view is very incomplete and it leaves out the side of any business activities that have to do with experience, judgment, heart, and quite frankly other hard-to-characterize – but very, very important – components of successful activities."

Secondly, Treacy claimed that reengineering from its birth has been inseparable from the word "radical." He said, "That has a lot to do with the fact that the principal proselytizer Michael Hammer – much like Gary Hamel by the way – believes in a big radical change. And the result is that a great number of reengineering initiatives, while they're exciting on paper, are abject failures when it comes to implementation, because frankly people try to bite off more than what they can chew."

Dr. Treacy's view reflects that of many executives on the topic of reengineering and this is linked to their view on process in general. Consequently, many leaders still fail to appreciate fully that the benefits of process thinking go far beyond the realm of simple cost reduction to a broad range of management topics, including strategy, engagement, leadership, growth, mergers, and acquisitions.

The way leaders have chosen to interpret the definition of process is part of the reason for the prevailing narrow view of process. The technical definition of "process" has remained fairly static over the years. Davenport wrote in 1993, "In definitional terms, a process is simply a structured, measured set of activities designed to produce a specific output for a particular customer or market."[5] Hammer wrote in 2001, "Process is a technical term with a precise definition: an organized group of related activities that together create a result of value to the customer."[6] While technically correct, neither of these definitions sufficiently predisposes leaders to emphasize the enterprise view of process in a value chain context, where the flow of activities across groups, functions, or departments in creating value for customers is what counts. Even though both authors emphasize that processes are all about delivering results for customers, many leaders have elected to interpret process in a narrow sense, even to the point of limiting it to the activities within a given group, department, or function. Only after overcoming the trap sprung by this narrow functional view can one begin to see the big picture of how a company's processes is how it gets the work done.

A shift in conventional wisdom is needed to accommodate a broader, more comprehensive, systemic view of the business in a process context. One definition of process management that adopts a systemic view is that process management at the enterprise level involves "the deliberative, collaborative, and increasingly technology-aided definition, improvement and management of a firm's enterprise business processes."[7]

But you will have to prepare yourself to accept this broader view of process. There are two things you can do in this regard. First, meet with your customers, and talk to them about how your company is performing and how they use your product or service. Don't do it over the phone. As Le Carre wrote, "A desk is a dangerous place from which to watch the world."[8] Candid dialogue with your customers will lead you to discover the importance of cross-functional and cross-group collaboration and interdependence. Then, as Shapiro, et al, advised, you might "staple yourself to an order."[9] By so doing you can view first hand the flow of work involved in delivering products or services to customers.

An indispensable element here is the disciplined measurement of how your business is doing in meeting customer requirements. Only by looking at the business from the customer's point of view and measuring how you are doing in terms of the timeliness, quality, and cost of products and services provided to customers, can you become clear on the true nature of the firm's performance.

Once you have opened your mind to thinking about process at the enterprise level as the means by which your company creates value for customers and gets results, you will find that the process view on topics such as strategy and growth become more meaningful. The following provides some insight on the nature of the needed shift in conventional wisdom as it relates to a broad range of critical management practices, including strategy formulation and implementation, leadership, employee engagement, growth, and mergers.

Strategy

What is more important, strategy or execution? Of course, that's a trick question for you. Obviously both are crucial. Yet, when Fortune magazine ran an article in 1999 that included the statement, "In the majority of cases, we estimate 70 percent – the real problem isn't bad strategy...it's bad execution," it attracted a lot of attention. More recently, the general view appears to be that "execution" is more important than "strategy," as Sir John Bond expressed in his view on the state of affairs in the financial services sector by saying, "There are few original strategies in banking. There is only execution."[10]

What has not been fully appreciated is this: A clear compelling articulation of strategic direction is a necessary but insufficient condition for disciplined, flawless execution. Likewise, a robust process view of the business is a necessary, but insufficient condition for disciplined, flawless execution.

Conventional wisdom says you can't execute flawlessly in the absence of clear strategy. The shift in conventional wisdom is that you can't do it in the absence of a process view of the business on an end-to-end basis.

It's somewhat puzzling why more business leaders have not nurtured the mental models and behaviors needed to define strategy in a business process, value chain context.

After all, many would agree that it is the set of enterprise business processes which define how work is done and creates value for customers and shareholders. The academic community has been promoting this point of view for some time now. As far back as 1985, Dr. Michael Porter emphasized the concept of the value chain and noted, "Activities, then, are the basics of competitive advantage. Overall advantage or disadvantage results from all of a company's activities, not only a few" and then went on to say, "The essence of strategy is choosing to perform activities differently than rivals do."[11]

Both a clear definition of the firm's core processes and a shared understanding of the process framework are needed in order for a firm's leaders to answer questions such as "What core processes are critical?" It's also important to bear in mind that at the enterprise level, the effective application of process thinking is not limited simply to the traditional linear view of process – converting inputs to outputs. Instead, the focus is on the flow of activities as they cross-organizational boundaries in order to maximize whatever level of speed, and what level of quality is needed to create the value that will satisfy customers and provide customers with "more for less." So why don't more organizations express the firm's strategy in process terms?

Again, the culprit is the traditional functional mindset. This is manifest in two ways. First, many leaders are not accustomed to thinking in process terms at the enterprise level. Instead, they view processes at a micro level, more like procedures. Perhaps this point was best expressed by the vice president from a major chemical company. In response to the question, "Does process thinking come into play in formulating strategy?" he answered,

> Not top of the mind, I would say. When I think of process, I think of something that's providing a systematic reproducibility, in spite of changes in people. It provides me with a sense of relief that I don't have anything to worry about. So normally you end up associating process with something that is cumbersome, something that is rigid. Most of the time I'm pleased with the existence of processes, sporadically, I loathe them – you are more apt to hear that the process doesn't allow something as opposed to saying that, sure, we can handle that special request easily.

The signs are clear when leaders view processes as procedures. You are apt to hear people say, "Process slows us down" or "Process reduces our flexibility and creativity." Whenever this distorted view of process exists, it may be challenging to raise the level of thinking of the leadership team to pay attention to the firm's large, cross-functional business processes.

Next, the traditional functional mindset reinforces the status quo in strategy development. For years, many firms have done the same thing, over and over again, in formulating strategy. When the time comes for a company to develop its strategic plan, the leadership team goes on a "strategic retreat." There they debate and discuss all the typical questions which traditionally need to be answered to formulate strategy. These will typically include questions such as: What are our fundamental values and beliefs? What products and services will we offer? What customer groups will we serve? What will fuel our growth? What will cause us to succeed? What financial and non-financial results will we achieve? What strategic initiatives must we do well at?

Then the leadership team returns to the day-to-day task of running the business and staff prepares a binder with the key findings and plans from the strategic retreat. A few weeks later, the binder is complete and the leadership team assigns accountability for the strategic initiatives to department heads.

But here is the fly in the ointment. The execution of strategy relies upon the improvement and management of the firm's large, cross-functional business processes – not upon actions taken in isolation by department heads. A static, departmentalized view of strategy leads to "me-too" strategies and the use of old, worn out phrases in articulating strategic direction.

What's needed is a more holistic view of the enterprise that acknowledges the inherent complexity of business and the central role of business processes. One such view is presented by Alan Brache in *How Organizations Work: Taking a Holistic Approach to Enterprise Health.*[12] Brache draws a parallel between human wellness and organizational wellness. He explores key elements of organization health, revealing the extent of interdependence, and the ways to assess them. The key elements include the external environment, leadership, strategy, business processes, goals and measurement, human capabilities, knowledge management, organizational structure, and culture. Aptly, the role of business processes is positioned as essential to overall performance.

If you agree with the potential benefit of viewing the business in process terms, then you will appreciate that taking action to understand the firm's performance in meeting customer requirements should actually precede strategy formulation, and not be treated as an after thought. In essence, it should be a part of the "environmental scan" that establishes the baseline for current performance and provides the foundation for decisions around the size of the performance gap.

Then the key discussions in strategy formulation would relate to a process context. In this manner, the major strategic initiatives could then be framed in terms of the company's end-to-end processes in order to facilitate implementation. The shift in conventional wisdom as it pertains to management practice in strategy formulation and implementation is summarized in Table 2.1 below.

Area	Conventional Practice	Progressive Practice
Preparation	▪ Environmental Scan focuses solely on traditional external and internal factors	▪ Environmental Scan includes an assessment of how the company is performing for customers
Strategy Formulation	▪ Driven by tradition, involves mainly small, incremental changes	▪ Customer centric focus, process is a distinct part of the context
Strategy Implementation	▪ Accountability for strategic initiatives is assigned to department heads	▪ Accountability for strategic initiatives explicitly acknowledges the need for cross-functional collaboration

Table 2.1. Shifting Conventional Wisdom: Strategy

It is the power of process thinking that enables firms to answer the questions, "Which of our key processes need to be improved, and by how much, in order to perform for our customers?" In turn, this prepares the organization to then ask and answer, "Which of our key processes need to be improved, and by how much, in order to achieve our strategic goals?" That's what enables execution.

It is the answer to these questions that pays significant dividends in terms of linking strategy to execution and has considerable benefits in more broadly engaging the entire organization in executing on strategy, as discussed below.

Engagement

Conventional wisdom states that a firm needs to engage its employees in order to execute strategy. The desirable shift in conventional wisdom is that process thinking can provide the needed context to engage the entire organization.

Engaging the entire organization in the execution of strategy is another topic that has attracted increasing interest. Leaders are beginning to recognize that the old worn-out phrases such as "We are dedicated to growth" and "We will put customers first" simply do not provide sufficient guidance to employees on what they can do to execute strategy. More specifically, it doesn't help employees understand how the things they do on a daily basis will contribute to the achievement of the organization's overall strategy.

The majority of the firm's employees are involved in activities such as developing products or services, selling these offerings, delivering them, and servicing them, etc. These activities are actually performed through collaborative cross-functional activities – or business processes – if you will.

By articulating strategic objectives in terms of the specific improvement needed for these cross-functional activities, leaders can create context for the firm's major initiatives. This creates the means to engage and even inspire employees to action. Just consider the simple example in Table 2.2. Which statement in this table is more likely to engage, inspire, and lead to clear accountability?

The Traditional Perspective	The Process Perspective
▪ Customer service is our top priority.	▪ We will improve our performance by delivering 98.8% of orders on time, accurately, and complete, with no backorders.

Table 2.2. Two Perspectives

People value plain speaking and simple, clear goals and priorities that make sense to them in their roles within the firm.

For example, the leader of a global specialty chemicals business articulated the purpose of his firm as providing "value beyond the product." This statement was supported by a "customer bill of rights" that specified that the firm is committed to providing customers with:

- what they ordered
- delivery at the time they asked for it to be delivered
- complete, accurate, and defect-free deliveries
- an accurate, complete, and timely invoice

Now, that's clear isn't it? We should never forget that people have difficulty in identifying their role in delivering on the traditional financial measures of performance such as profit margin, cash flow, and asset intensity. Measuring what counts for customers is the essential ingredient of process management and provides a more relevant mechanism to engage people in the organization and build a culture of discipline. People perform work. Work is process. Thus, putting critical initiatives in process terms makes it much easier for people to understand what it is they do and how it is important to the customer and, ultimately, to the company and its shareholders.

The engagement and teamwork-related benefits of viewing the business in process terms has been known for some time now. Øystein Risan, the Operations Director for NSB, the Norwegian national railway company, described the benefits of taking a business process view as follows:

> We have a much more united unit. Everyone, the drivers, conductors, management, the union has a more common understanding of what we are trying to do – and that we are all doing our best to achieve it. And people actually believe that each individual makes a difference and that small improvements every day will eventually end up being massive improvements. On any objective measure, punctuality, cost efficiency, safety, you'll see huge improvements.

And I think it's about believing that you can make a little change and you'll get huge end results.

Ed Maggio, the Vice President of Operations for RSA Security articulated the benefit of looking at the business in process terms:

It gets people focused on improvement, it gives them a better understanding of what the process is, it gives them a venue for coming up with ideas on improvement, it gives them ownership of their processes and ability to change their processes, and it gives them ownership of the results, metrics of that process, and the achievement of high-performance metrics.

Jim Collins, in *Good to Great,* points out that a "culture of discipline" is not about control or bureaucracy.[13] The impetus for broad based engagement needs to start at the top and has much to do with establishing accountability for performance for everyone. That is part of the key to engagement, and that is what the deliberate and collaborative management of a firm's end-to-end business processes can enable.

Leadership

One of the more common criticisms of leaders by their employees is that they really don't know the business – at least not at the right level of detail.

Conventional wisdom states that leadership is essential to overall corporate performance. The shift in conventional wisdom is that the power of process thinking at the enterprise level can enable leadership.

In the bestselling book, *Execution: The Discipline of Getting Things Done,* Bossidy and Charan describe seven essential leadership behaviors, including: know your people and your business, insist on realism, set clear goals and priorities, and reward the doers.[14] To illustrate the potential power of process in enabling leadership, just consider how process principles and practices can positively influence several of these essential behaviors:

Knowing the business involves understanding in some detail

the flow of work and the roles of key departments and key people as work crosses traditional organizational boundaries; only then can executives have sufficient knowledge to deliver best value to customers and shareholders. Many executives do not appreciate the workflow at a sufficient level of detail, and that lack of understanding can detract from how value is created for customers. That is where business process definition and management comes into play, for it requires a certain depth of involvement in the workflow. In some cases, it is important for executives to understand the details themselves. In others, it will be sufficient to have an appreciation for what is involved and engage the individuals who do the work on a daily basis to understand the "devil in the details."

Whether it is to develop new products or deliver "perfect orders," to deliver value to customers, an organization and its leaders must excel at managing and improving the flow of work that crosses functional boundaries. For example, to deliver "perfect orders," a firm must improve and manage the entire flow of work in the so-called "order fulfillment process," from receipt of order to receipts of product or service by the customer. This flow of work crosses traditional organizational boundaries, and that is the challenge for firms that still cling to a traditional functional paradigm. It is the challenge that leaders can address through process thinking.

By looking at the business from the customer's point of view and measuring performance in terms of the timeliness, quality, and cost of products and services provided to customers, executives become better equipped to insist on realism. After all, that is precisely what customers care about – a flawless product delivered on time, complete, and defect free; they have no personal interest in how a firm is organized.

The business process view also assists executives in setting clear, realistic goals and priorities. When leaders wish to engage employees as willing followers it is worthwhile remembering that people value plain speaking. They appreciate the clear goals and priorities that process thinking enables and the guidance it provides with respect to their roles within the context of the firm.

Another of the potential benefits of perceiving the business in the context of its cross-functional business processes has to do with rewarding the people and teams of people who get things done for customers. This is frequently difficult when the workflow is considered one piece at a time. Expressing priorities in broad, cross-functional process terms can be instrumental in acknowledging the people from different departments who collaborate to make significant contributions to the creation of value for customers in observable, measurable terms.

Some leaders already recognize that the power of process thinking at the enterprise level can enable leadership. They just express it in their own way. Here is how Jim Conway, the former COO of the Dana Farber Cancer Institute, said it:

> In health care – we all have a responsibility for the whole process – no matter where we sit in the process. ... I think leaders have to be looking at the whole system and not just the pieces – it's back to this institutional approach. Breaking down silos. Turning tables. Working together.

That's leadership. Breaking down silos. Working together. The needed shift in conventional wisdom involves the profound understanding that the power of process thinking at the enterprise level can enable leadership.

Growth

Conventional wisdom says that growth is essential to overall business performance. The shift in conventional wisdom is the less well-known fact that process thinking is essential to growth.

Michael Treacy emphasized in *Double-Digit Growth* that most management teams are adept at meeting cost targets or shaving 10% from the expense base or improving an individual process – but are far less able to plan and execute double-digit growth. Why is that? Treacy argues that firms often lack the tools and management disciplines to tackle growth in a structured, systematic way.[15] Certainly that's part of the answer.

But the other part is this. Rapid, sustainable growth requires not just a systematic approach but also a systemic view and broad cross-functional collaboration – and that is something many firms continue to struggle with. That's precisely where process thinking comes into play.

A process focus on items such as flawless delivery and "first time right" responsiveness is essential in providing existing products or services to either existing or new markets.

Of course, that is not all there is to fueling growth. A firm can have outstanding performance in terms of delivery and responsiveness and yet fail to grow because the features of its product or service no longer meet customer needs or the offering is priced well above competitive offerings.

But the converse is also true. Firms that have excellent products or services that are attractively priced and promoted can fail to grow due to sub-par performance in the delivery and service of their offerings.

Successful, sustainable growth demands that a firm measures, improves, and manages its performance with respect to at least two key processes – order fulfillment and new product or service development. To illustrate this, just consider Table 2.3 below, which depicts the typical options to organic growth via a product-market matrix.

Firms who excel at managing the performance of the "order fulfillment" or "order to cash" process will not only monitor how they are doing in terms of delivering "perfect orders," they will also pay attention to customer churn. While the measurement of customer churn is currently most common in the wireless telecommunications, the cable TV, and the financial services sectors, it will likely be adopted as a key metric in other sectors. As Michael Treacy emphasizes in *Double Digit Growth*, management teams should ask, "How much growth did customer churn cost your business last year?" But that's only the first question. The next questions are "What were the root causes of churn? What could we do to prevent churn? Which of our key activities contribute to and can help control churn?" This is where process thinking and acting come into play as the most effective means to conduct diagnostics on the impact and mitigation of customer churn.

Market	Existing Product /Service	New Product/Service
Existing Market	▪ Flawless product /service delivery	▪ Flawless new product /service introduction AND ▪ Flawless product /service delivery
New Market	▪ Flawless product /service delivery	▪ Flawless new product/service introduction AND ▪ Flawless product /service delivery

Table 2.3. Growth Options

When it comes to organic growth, be it based on selling more of existing products or services or introducing new products or services, the systematic improvement and management of the order fulfillment and new product development processes and a systemic view of the business are essential. That calls for a shift in conventional wisdom such that process performance is acknowledged as essential to growth.

This applies equally to the development and introduction of new products or services to either existing or new markets. Here the firm's aptitude in new product/service commercialization comes into play, in addition to flawless delivery and "first time right" responsiveness.

In the 1993 book, *Winning at New Products*, Robert Cooper outlines how a handful of companies (about 22% of firms surveyed) are able to generate nearly 50% of sales and profits from new products. This level of performance is about twice as high as that experienced by the other 78% of respondents in the survey.[16]

Why this marked difference? Again, part of the answer is to be found in the broad, cross-functional nature of new product development and introduction.

Since as far back as 1993, the process itself has been well documented. At that time, Robert Cooper developed the now well-known Stage-Gate® process depicted in Figure 2.1.

This is essentially a conceptual and operational road map for moving a new product project from idea to launch; it divides the effort into distinct stages divided by management decision gates.

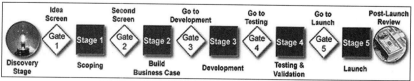

Figure 2.1. The Stage-Gate Process[17]

Successful new product development requires cross-departmental teams to complete a prescribed set of related cross-functional tasks in each stage prior to obtaining management approval to proceed to the next stage of product development. And there's the rub.

Again, the key concept is that in order to achieve successful new product development and commercialization, firms must measure and manage the performance of this large cross-functional process. It's equally important to have clarity on customer expectations and a mechanism for ongoing customer input.

Of course, organic or internally generated growth is not the only option. There is also growth through merger or acquisition, and that is addressed below.

Mergers and Acquisitions

Conventional wisdom states that mergers and acquisitions represent a significant means to fueling a company's growth. The needed shift in conventional wisdom is in realizing that the successful integration of a merged or acquired entity demands process thinking and acting.

It has been reported that up to 80% of mergers fail to reach their financial objectives. A large part of the reason for the failure of many mergers and acquisitions is the inability of the merged firm to perform for, and meet the needs of their customers. In part, this is related to the fact that newly merged firms often aggressively pursue merger synergies that were estimated in the pre-merger "due diligence" period. Understandably, the due diligence is customarily completed without much specific information on core processes and their relative health. A complicating factor is that the top team may elect to chase the originally estimated merger synergies via extreme cost cutting versus understanding how to achieve these synergies in the best way via business process improvement.

One of the more extreme examples of merger meltdown was the union of Union Pacific (UP) and Southern Pacific (SP) railroads. Shipments that were planned to take five days to reach their destinations often took as many as 30 – if they didn't get lost altogether. Overtaxed computer systems lost track of freight cars. Delivery bottlenecks were widespread – particularly in Houston, where freight snarls were reported to have lasted for a year and a half.[18]

It has taken over 8 years for the Union Pacific share price to reach the pre-merger level of about $70.00 per share.

In contrast, The Dow Chemical Company's acquisition of Union Carbide represents an example of how attention to the merged firm's end-to-end processes can be instrumental in effectively executing the integration phase of a merger and thereby performing for both customers and shareholders.

Of course, at the time of the deal Dow had learned from other failures such as the UP/SP debacle, and it had several months to focus on operational integration issues prior to the final deal being consummated. Nevertheless, Dow did many things right.

One of the critical success factors was the clarity of vision created by the joint Dow/ UCC Supply Chain integration team and repeatedly emphasized by Richard A. Gerardo, the then Vice President Global Supply Chain with Dow, as, "We will not give the customer a reasonable excuse to go elsewhere."

Pragmatically, Dow was committed to ensuring that the integration of the two firms was executed flawlessly. This meant that on

Day 1 of the merger and every day that follows:
- customer orders are taken,
- purchase orders are placed,
- goods are shipped and received,
- invoices are issued, and
- money is collected and bills are paid.

And all of the above had to be done safely, legally, and on time! Understanding the respective work processes of the two firms was central to the merger.

As Stephen Graham, Work Process and Technology Leader for Dow Supply Chain, outlined in a presentation at a November 2004 Brainstorm Group conference on BPM, the Dow focus was on satisfying customers first, then seeking to achieve the financial targets set by corporate leadership. This involved assembling cross-functional teams from both firms for order receipts and handling, logistics and transport, planning and scheduling, invoicing and payment collection, and regulatory affairs/compliance to assess, improve, and integrate the entire set of supply chain processes *on a global basis.*

Due to EU and SEC related delays, it was February 6, 2001, before the merger became effective. But, on Day 1 of merged operations Dow indeed:
- took and placed orders
- missed no shipments
- delayed no payments
- collected its money

And Dow was safe; and so was any community where Dow operated. There was a great deal more to Dow's success than just a process orientation. For example, the strong alignment among key members of management on what needed to be done, leadership's recognition of the need to avoid the pitfall of premature cost cutting, and the dedication to letting people know whether they had a job in the new entity were also critical success factors. But process did play a large part. Figure 2.2 represents an illustration of how the work activity continuum context was created for the Dow-Union Carbide integration.

Stephen Graham provided the following summary of the "musts" which contributed to Dow's success:

- Documented task level work processes as a reference
- Mandate for action
- Align to strategy of Company / Function/ Business
- Leadership at all levels: executive, program, sub process
- You don't need tools – you need great people and belief

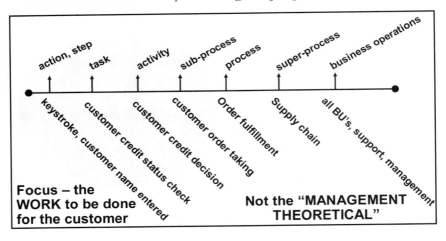

Figure 2.2. Dow-Union Carbide Integration[19]

Success in M&A integration is not just about a process view. It is unlikely that Dow could have achieved a successful integration without the top-to-bottom alignment driven by the leadership team and management's readiness to face up to the "show me the money quick" pressures that many companies face in similar circumstances.

Summary

In a recent special for public television, *The Power of Intention*, best-selling author and speaker Dr. Wayne Dyer emphasized, "When you change the way you look at things – the things you look at change."

Now, Dr. Dyer was not talking about business processes or even business in general. Instead, his aim was to provide guidance on how everyone can connect to his or her own infinite potential.

But the message applies equally to business. How you look at things matters! Indeed, whether it is in our personal lives or in the life of a complex business, the right perspective changes everything. That is why a shift in conventional wisdom and a new view of leadership mindset and executive behaviors is an essential part of the journey for companies who want to leverage the organization's capability to provide customers with "more for less."

What's Needed	Signs of Progress
A shift in conventional wisdom with respect to: ▪ Strategy ▪ Engagement ▪ Leadership ▪ Growth ▪ M&A integration	There are signs of progress when you: ▪ Measure what matters to customers ▪ Contemplate defining strategic initiatives in terms of the performance of the enterprise level business processes ▪ Think about rewarding people and teams of people for their contribution in improving performance for customers

Table 2.4. Signs of Progress

This shift in conventional wisdom is just the beginning. It is closely tied to measuring what matters to customers. How can you tell whether you are making progress? Table 2.4 illustrates.

Shifting conventional wisdom simply prepares leaders to contemplate what's involved in creating an enterprise view of the business in a process context. Then the task of developing the right mindset, behaviors, and skills to improve and manage the company's key business processes in a value chain context, so as to perform for customers, begins in earnest.

Chapter 2: Self Assessment Questions

1. Does your firm begin the strategy process with an understanding of customer expectations?
2. Is your strategy expressed in terms that people at various levels throughout the organization can understand?
3. Do your leaders understand how work flows across the traditional organizational boundaries? Do they "know the business" in this context and at the right level of detail?
4. Are there visible rewards and recognition for those people who are instrumental in improving the performance of the firm's large, cross-functional processes?
5. Do the firm's plans for growth include clear performance metrics for perfect order delivery and new product introduction?
6. Is the firm measuring the impact of customer churn? Do you have the means to identify the root causes of customer churn?
7. Do your M&A plans place significant emphasis on performing for customers on the first day of merged operations – and every day after?
8. Are your leaders more concerned about reporting relationships and authority than on the flow of work to create value for customers?
9. Is it common that executives and managers view the business with a functional bias?
10. To what extent is there a shared understanding of the business process view at the top team level?
11. Do people view processes on a micro level as procedures?
12. Do you hear complaints such as "process slows us down" or "process limits our creativity?"
13. Do leaders focus mainly on actual-to-budget metrics to assess progress?
14. Is goal setting a top down, unidirectional activity?
15. Are some executives visibly uncomfortable in meetings involving broad cross-department representatives?

References.

[1] Davenport, Thomas H., *Process Innovation*, Harvard Business School Press, 1993·

[2] Herbold, Robert J., *The Fiefdom Syndrome: The Turf Battles that Undermine Careers and Companies – and How to Overcome Them* , Currency, 2004

[3] Hammer, Michael, *The Agenda*, Crown Business, 2001.

[4] Ibid

[5] Ibid, page 5

[6] Ibid, page 53

[7] Spanyi, Andrew, 'Business Process Management is a Team Sport', Anclote Press, 2003.

[8] Le Carre, John, *The Honourable Schoolboy*, Knopf, 1977, page 84

[9] Shapiro, Benson P., and V. Rasturi Rangan and John J. Sviolka, 'Staple Yourself to An Order', *Harvard Business Review*, 1992

[10] Morais, Richard C., 'Bullterrier Banking', *Forbes Magazine*, July 24, 2000

[11] Porter, Michael, 'What is Strategy?', *Harvard Business Review*, November-December 1996.

[12] Brache, Alan P., *How Organizations Work: Taking a Holistic Approach to Enterprise Health*, Wiley, 2002

[13] Collins, Jim, *Good to Great*, Harper Business, 2001

[14] Bossidy, Larry and Ram Charan, *Execution: The Discipline of Getting Things Done*, Crown Business, 2002.

[15] Treacy, Michael, *Double-Digit Growth*, Portfolio, 2003

[16] Cooper, Robert G., *Winning at New Products: Accelerating the Process from Idea to Launch*, Perseus Books, 1993.

[17] http://www.prod-dev.com/stage-gate.shtml

[18] http://www.industryweek.com/CurrentArticles/asp/articles.asp?ArticleID=546

[19] Case Study: Process Thinking Applied to a Large Merger, Brainstorm Group Conference on BPM, 2004

Three

The Enterprise View

A picture is worth a thousand words.
– Napoleon Bonaparte

If the only picture you have of the firm is an organization chart, don't be surprised if that then dominates your leaders' view of the business and how they think about it.

How can a company realistically serve its customers if it doesn't even measure what matters most to them?

How can a company hope to provide their customer with "more for less" if it doesn't even have a schematic that puts the customer center stage and clearly depicts the company's activities in serving customers?

How can a company hope to perform for its customers if it does not put the right governance in place to assure clearly defined accountability for the flow of value added work that crosses traditional organizational boundaries?

The fact is that in spite of the rich body of literature that emerged on the topic of process during the eighties and nineties, relatively little has been written on ways firms can benefit from taking an enterprise view of corporate performance in process terms.

A number of firms have made significant progress in developing an enterprise view of the business in process terms. What's more, these firms appear to share a discrete set of characteristics that enable the development of this perspective. What follows provides insight on how you too can do it.

A Gap in the Literature

Just think about it. How many articles or books have you seen that provide guidance to leaders on a systemic, enterprise level view of applying process principles and practices?

Let's briefly consider the literature on process. Some maintain that the power of process thinking has been understood since the days of Frederick Taylor's 1911 publication, *Principles of Scientific Management*. The more common view is that the power of process to improve a firm's performance was broadly recognized in the era of the quality movement of the 1970s and 1980s through the writing of "quality" thought leaders, such as Deming, Juran, and Crosby.

In the 1990s, hot on the heels of the quality movement, Michael Hammer's HBR article "Reengineering Work: Don't Automate, Obliterate," argued against continuous, incremental improvement. Then, the 1993 book, *Reengineering the Corporation: A Manifesto for Business Revolution*, by Dr. Michael Hammer and James Champy, built on the concept of radical redesign or reengineering.

Dr. Thomas Davenport's 1993 book, *Process Innovation: Reengineering Work through Information Technology*, took a more balanced perspective on the radical improvement of business processes. Davenport stressed that business must not be viewed just in terms of functions, divisions, and products, but also as processes. He argued that process innovation initiatives are distinct from business-as-usual and require a project orientation, involving ad hoc, cross-functional project teams, and can lead to major reductions in process cost or time, or major improvements in quality, flexibility, service levels, or other business objectives. Yet he acknowledged that a firm that does not introduce continuous improvement after implementing process innovation is likely to revert to the old way of doing things. An important part of Davenport's contribution was his treatment of information technology.

One of the few examples of a systemic view of business in a process context was provided in Dr. Geary Rummler's and Alan Brache's book, *Improving Performance: How to Manage the White Space on the Organization Chart*, which appeared in 1990 and preceded the work of both Davenport and Hammer.

Rummler and Brache stressed both a systematic and a systemic view of organizations as complex systems. They argued that many executives simply do not understand, at a sufficient level of detail, how their firms develop, make, sell, and distribute products because their thinking is dominated by a traditional, departmental view. They provided readers with a practical framework on both process improvement and management. In that regard, their work was unique in that it provided useful frameworks for how to improve process performance, including a perspective on the organizational view, the process view, and job/performer view. This perspective was reinforced and updated by Paul Harmon in his 2003 book, *Business Process Change.*

In spite of a long history in the literature on the power of thinking in terms of process improvement, the practical focus by many organizations has been biased toward the understandable goal of reducing costs, or narrowly focused on individual business processes such as order entry, billing, procurement, and so on. Additionally, many process improvement efforts have targeted processes, which, for the most part, were contained within a single business function, thereby failing to capture the synergies inherent in examining the flow of work across multiple functions.

To this day, the power of process thinking when applied to the enterprise level is much less widely understood or practiced, even though researchers such as Dr. Kevin McCormack have begun to assemble quantitative evidence to show that the development of business process orientation in an organization will lead to positive outcomes from an overall business performance perspective.[1]

The criticism levied by Rummler and Brache way back in 1990 that "Many managers don't understand their business," unfortunately still holds true. That's because while leaders and managers may know much about the traditional business elements, "they often do not understand at a sufficient level of detail, how their businesses get products developed, made, sold, and distributed."[2]

If you agree that it's time for a change, then you need a framework for action in process terms to help you improve and manage the flow of cross-departmental activities that create value for customers. The key elements of this framework include a shared understanding of:

- the critical enterprise level business processes that create value;
- the critical few measures that define performance;
- a plan for improving and managing enterprise level business processes;
- accountability for results; and
- a communication plan that inspires and moves people to action.

Key Characteristics

Some firms will find it easier to create a framework for action than others. In the approach of firms such as Air Products, The Dow Chemical Company, Caterpillar Inc., Infosys, Nokia, and Xerox it is clear that there were certain common characteristics that facilitated the adoption of a business process focus. The characteristics these firms appear to have in common include:

- a long history of process improvement,
- a keen focus on customer satisfaction,
- a CEO with passion around the potential role of process improvement and management in creating value for both customers and shareholders,
- concern around the challenge of growth or an imminent competitive threat, and
- a certain degree of cultural fit.

To illustrate the importance of these characteristics, consider the case of Air Products, and then that of Nokia, outlined below.

Air Products and Chemicals, Inc. was founded in 1940. It had enjoyed healthy growth for 60 years when John P. Jones was appointed Chairman and CEO in 2000. Jones, intent on developing a plan for even greater growth and profitability, saw much inefficiency in Air Products' business. For one thing, people placed undue emphasis on "my business" and "my function" as opposed to a focus on satisfying customers. To redress these failings, Jones introduced a vision of the future called "Deliver the Difference," which was intended to coalesce the organization into a "one company" focus. Concurrently, Jones introduced four company-wide initiatives he believed were necessary to create and sustain increased shareholder, customer, and employee value. These were:

- Change – visibly value people in a positive work environment
- Portfolio Management – continuously improve the return on capital
- Growth – grow through innovation and superior products and services for customers
- Work processes – reduce costs through work process simplification

The fact that a process focus was one of these four initiatives is significant. Of course, Air Products had a long history of quality and process improvement dating back to the 1980s. Also, there was a good cultural fit for a process approach. There was a strong chemical engineering culture within Air Products that accepted and valued the merits of process thinking.

Over time, Air Products developed an Enterprise Process Blueprint that represented a view of its critical business processes, the key performance metrics, and facilitated the assignment of accountability for monitoring process performance. Figure 3.1 presents the Air Products Enterprise Process Blueprint. Given that supply chain concepts are central to success in the chemical industry, it makes sense that this "blueprint" was influenced by the Supply Chain Council's SCOR framework.

The Air Products Enterprise Process Blueprint employs the convention of using a single word to name each of the enterprise processes. With the exception of the "Build" process, most of the other enterprise processes could apply to almost any firm. In the Air Products context, the Align process sits on top of the seven customer-facing processes and the five supporting or enabling processes. It encompasses the development of the firm's short and long term plans, including mergers and acquisitions.

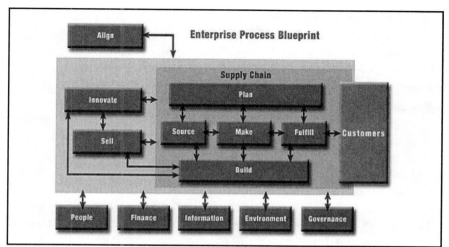

Figure 3.1. The Air Products Enterprise Process Blueprint

While Air Products had all the characteristics needed to facilitate an enterprise-wide process focus, it would not have happened without the recognition that this would contribute to increased shareholder, customer, and employee value. As Bill Cantwell, Vice President of Supply Chain said in a recent APQC report, "Creating a process-focused organization must be in the context of something that is very important to the company. A process-focused organization for the sake of being process focused has little value and, quite frankly, has a negative feel to it. If it is not placed within the context of strategy and the direction of the company, you are probably not going to get a whole lot of recognition or buy-in for the concept itself."

Air Products recognized that accountability for process performance, a concise and customer centric set of metrics, availability of supporting education and training, and alignment of information technology deployment were all needed to sustain the enterprise process focus. It is doubtful whether all of this could have been done in the absence of Air Products' long history of safety, and quality and process improvement.

Air Products appears to have had in place a broad range of the major characteristics which enable the development of a an enterprise view on process terms, including a long history of process improvement, a keen focus on customer satisfaction, a CEO with passion for the potential role of process improvement and management, concern for the challenge of growth or an imminent competitive threat, and a degree of cultural fit.

The case of Nokia provides another example of an organization that appears to have made progress on managing its enterprise level processes and shares several of these same characteristics.

Although the roots of Nokia go back as far as 1865, the Nokia Corporation was actually founded in 1967. In the 1980s, Nokia acquired a number of firms including Mobira, Salora, Televa, and Luxor of Sweden, the consumer electronics operations and part of the component business of the German Standard Elektrik Lorenz, the French consumer electronics company, Oceanic, and the Swiss cable machinery company, Maillefer.

In addition to these acquisitions, in the late 1980s, Nokia became the largest Scandinavian information technology company through the acquisition of Ericsson's data systems division and also acquired the Dutch cable company, NKF. Since the beginning of the 1990s, Nokia has concentrated on its current core business, telecommunications, by divesting its information technology and basic industry operations.

Nokia has had a longstanding focus on quality and process improvement, and the firm grew significantly in the 1990s, largely through its new product introduction capability and also its focus on logistics processes to improve the Demand Supply Network Performance. In the late 1990s Nokia's leadership in new product introduction began to be challenged by other mobile phone competitors.

Around 2001-2002, Nokia started to seek growth from new emerging trends. These included accelerating demand for consumer multimedia, rapid growth in emerging markets, recovering Enterprise markets and growth in 3G commercialization. Process thinking has been part of the Nokia heritage. Indeed, as Timo Raikaslehto, acting Vice President, Quality, said, "We have a long history of process management, with good support to the current core business; now the focus needs to be extended to the new areas in our business."

The combination of a longstanding focus on quality and process improvement, a culture open to thinking in process terms, and competitive pressures combined to drive the development of an enterprise level view of business processes at Nokia. The firm has defined its business processes on an enterprise level, as depicted in Figure 3.2, and these apply to each of its four business groups: Mobile Phones, Multimedia, Enterprise Solutions, and Networks.

Further, Nokia has clearly defined the accountability for the performance of its core processes. Timo Raikaslehto explained,

> First of all we have at the Nokia level owners, one executive who owns each of those four processes, then in addition, we have a Nokia process owner for each of these core processes, then at the business group level we have the business owners for these processes. So it's kind of a networked organization, and the requirements for process development come from the business organizations.

> Naturally our core processes are on different maturity levels due to the fact that their development history is different. The product creation process, with the longest background, is being renewed, while, for example, some parts of the customer engagement process are just taking their first steps on the Nokia level. There, the processes have been traditionally developed as close to the customer interface as possible; now some see a need for commonalization and standardization as our customers are becoming more global.

Nokia's focus on measurement is closely tied to the definition of its core processes. It regularly monitors performance on metrics such as trade customer satisfaction, end user satisfaction, field failure rate, manufacturing failure rate, milestone hit rate, time to concept time, and on-time delivery to request.

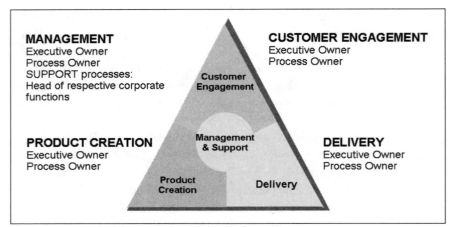

Figure 3.2. Nokia's Core Processes

In addition to having certain characteristics which facilitate the development of an enterprise focus on process performance, both Air Products' and Nokia's progress can also be attributed to their appreciation for the importance of closely integrating process thinking with strategy, establishing accountability for process performance, and defining key measures.

Does your company have what it takes to begin the journey in developing an enterprise view of the business in process terms? Is there a long history of process improvement? Do leaders share a keen focus on customer satisfaction? Does your CEO have passion for the potential role of process improvement and management in creating value for both customers and shareholders? Is there keen concern for the challenge of growth or an imminent competitive threat? Do you think there is a reasonable degree of cultural fit?

If so, then there's value in considering how actually to create a customer-centric process view of the business and make it work for you. Although some aspects may still pose a challenge, here are a few concepts to consider.

Creating a Framework for Action

The first step in creating a framework for action is to define and depict the critical few enterprise level business processes that create value for the firm and its customers. A picture is worth a thousand words.

You cannot buy or borrow an enterprise level process schematic if you want to develop a shared understanding of how value is created and what are the critical interdependencies of departments. You have to build it – by yourselves – although you can get some thought provoking ideas from the reference sources briefly described in Appendix A.

To begin, look at the business from the customer's point of view. This will help change the typical inside-out view of the business that the traditional, functional paradigm promotes, and seeing from the customer's point of view will help you identify the critical measures of performance that reflect the customer's particular requirements.

Then, try not to call the end-to-end processes by the same name that you use in describing internal departments. This, too, will assist in shifting mindset – new names for seeing things in new ways.

Next, be clear on the definition of each end-to-end process: Clarify where the process starts, the key steps in the process, the departments involved, the output, and the major measures of process performance.

Get your hands dirty. Sure, it's OK to assign a group of internal experts to prepare a "draft" process schematic for review and refinement by the top team. But beware of outsourcing this activity to outsiders as it may adversely affect the degree of buy-in and ownership at the top team level.

Then, do it quickly. Don't take weeks or months hoping to get it perfect. It will never be perfect. A few weeks of data gathering and a couple of days off-site is often enough to develop a workable model that will serve as a basis for next steps.

Finally, do not underestimate the importance of gaining a shared understanding and a deep commitment to the process view of how the organization works. Even those companies who have made good progress on improving some of their end-to-end business processes struggle with top team buy-in to the process perspective in the absence of an enterprise level schematic. To illustrate, consider the comments of the vice-president of operations at a company that has made significant progress in improving its order fulfillment process. When asked "to what extent is there a shared understanding of the business process view at the top team level?" he said:

> I would say that it's about a 30 percent penetration. I think there's some understanding of it, but I think it still reverts back to the siloed concept at various levels. When you get to the upper levels, the executive levels of the company, it's like OK – so that's what happens inside this operational financial space, so if I'm in engineering, I don't really have to worry about that. And you may choose to do that, and that's an initiative you're spending time on, well – we've got other initiatives that we're working on.

Some organizations have found that there is value in using available reference frameworks to conduct education at the top team level prior to embarking on the development of their own company's enterprise view schematic. Valuable reference frameworks of the process view at a high level are available from sources such as The American Productivity & Quality Center (APQC), The MIT Process Handbook, and The Supply Chain Council. A brief discussion of the use of these reference frameworks is included as Appendix A.

The APQC's high-level model can be useful to stimulate thought at the top team level. The first version of the Process Classification Framework (PCF) was developed in 1993, and the current 2005 version is depicted in the table below. The PCF was developed by APQC and member companies as an "open standard" to facilitate improvement through process management and benchmarking. The PCF organizes operating and management processes into 12 enterprise-level categories, including process groups and over 1,500 processes and associated activities.

Operating Processes	Management and Support Services
1. Develop Vision And Strategy	6. Develop and Manage Human Capital
2. Design And Develop Products And Services	7. Manage Information Technology
3. Market And Sell Products And Services	8. Manage Financial Resources
4. Deliver Products And Services	9. Acquire, Construct and Manage Property
5. Manage Customer Service	10. Manage Environmental Health and Safety
	11. Manage External Relationships
	12. Manage Knowledge, Improvement and Change

Table 3.1. The APQC PFC Components

Some firms have found the APQC PCF language to be too functional in nature. This criticism is that the names of the PCF processes sound too much like the work done by traditional departments, such as Marketing, Sales, and Finance, for there to be a fundamental shift in thinking about the business. Another criticism of this framework is that the names of the processes are not sufficiently concise and precise.

Yet, other firms have found it expedient to adopt the APQC PCF with only minor refinements. Xerox is one firm that did just that. As George Maszle, Director, Xerox Lean Six Sigma Deployment, explained, "In the past we spent a lot of time debating the process framework, so when we re-implemented the process hierarchy with Xerox Lean Six Sigma, we adopted the APQC structure. With a few minor changes this satisfied our needs just fine." The components of the high-level Xerox process framework are depicted in Table 3.2 below.

Not only did Xerox find the APQC PCF useful at a high level, but also the underlying details of each macro process block available in the PCF document facilitated its efforts such that Lean Six Sigma projects could be searched on, based on the different subprocesses.

Operating Processes	Management and Support Processes
1. Understand Markets and Customers 2. Develop Vision and Strategy 3. Develop Products and Services 4. Market 5. Sell 6. Produce and Deliver Products 7. Produce and Deliver Services 8. Invoice Customers and Collects Payments 9. Service and Support Customers	10. Develop and Manage Human Resources 11. Manage Information Resources 12. Manage Financial and Physical Resources 13. Execute Compliance and Ethics Programs 14. Manage External Relationships 15. Manage Improvement and Change

Table 3.2. Xerox Corporation's Processes[3]

Not only did Xerox find the APQC PCF useful at a high level, but also the underlying details of each macro process block available in the PCF document facilitated its efforts such that Lean Six Sigma projects could be searched on, based on the different sub-processes.

The Xerox experience is a concrete example of how the use of reference models can stimulate leadership thinking. What is significant here is that Xerox took the time to refine the APQC PCF such that it accurately reflected its own business. That's essential and brings us to a note of caution in the use of reference models:

Do you remember the last time that a friend or colleague showed you a picture of his or her children? Do you remember smiling politely at picture after picture? There's a meaningful parallel with reference models: Like pictures of other people's children they are interesting but not necessarily relevant. That's why it is so important to invest the time and energy in refining a reference model to make it your own, and to achieve relevance and shared understanding.

Measuring What Matters

Once the top team has reached a shared understanding on the components of its own enterprise level process model, the next step is to do the same for the firm's current level of performance on a few critical metrics. This typically involves getting real data on a set of measures around the timeliness, quality, and cost of product or service delivery and other key aspects of the firm, such as developing new products or services.

One might think that getting data on the firm's current performance would be easy. In reality, it can be quite problematic. While most companies have extensive data on revenues, margins, earnings, and cash flow, in contrast the data on factors such as on-time delivery, accuracy, responsiveness, and completeness is sometimes difficult to assemble.

You'll certainly need the assistance of internal staff, but your guiding principle should still be, "Do it yourselves and do it quickly." Use sampling techniques whenever data isn't readily available from existing information systems. Note that sampling doesn't need to be a time-consuming, academic exercise. Simply capturing a couple dozen data points will help estimate current performance to a "good enough" level.

Assembling this type of current performance data is doubly valuable. First, it facilitates an objective and shared view of how the firm is performing when set against customer requirements. Second, it sets the baseline for the subsequent assessment of the size of the gap between current level of performance and desired level of performance.

But beware. At the top team level, there are two major pitfalls to avoid as you attempt to reach some shared understanding of how the firm is performing against customer requirements. The first of these is a natural tendency, in measuring what customers really want, to either gloss over the facts or take the easy way out. It's easy to focus on the firm's ability to meet "the promised date" for product or service delivery, rather than zeroing-in on what customers really want, which is meeting "the requested date." The typical cop-out comment by leaders in this respect is that "our customers' request dates are frequently unreasonable."

A corporate decision to focus solely on corporate performance in meeting the delivery dates it has promised to customers often takes a firm down a slippery slope of self-satisfaction, complacency, denial, and self-delusion. To adopt such an attitude is to take yet another small step toward saying that the firm should be satisfied with 95% performance against its own promised dates. That this would mean breaking its promise to its customers in five out of one hundred instances is swept under the executive rug. Firms dedicated to candor in measurement will want to track both sets of metrics – performance versus promised date, and performance versus requested date.

The second pitfall encountered in reaching a shared understanding of how the firm is performing against customer requirements is far more subtle and, therefore, more problematic. It typically starts when one or several members of the leadership team vehemently challenge the validity of the data on current performance, and then acquiesce in the face of feedback from the majority of the leadership team, while never truly accepting the data on estimated current performance. This lack of buy-in is difficult to assess and even more complex to address. The problems it creates can only be truly observed much later – in the form of silent, stoic resistance. To mitigate this, it is useful for the leader to ask each member of the top team to articulate his or her acceptance of the data on current performance.

The Process Management Plan

Once a shared understanding of the definition of the firm's enterprise level business processes and its current performance has been achieved, the top team can then proceed to build a plan that will improve and manage the firm's large, cross-functional business processes.

Such a plan needs to answer two fundamental questions: Which of our business processes need to be improved, and by how much, in order to achieve our strategic objectives? Who will be held accountable for this planned improvement and performance management?

Some firms find it useful to prepare a working document prior to convening the top team. Table 3.3 illustrates the working document for a hypothetical office services company, which outlines the key components on a single page.

Business Process	Input(s)	Key Steps	Output(s)	Functions Involved	Measures
Promote	Growth strategies Budgets	Plan Implement Assess	Inquiries Orders	Marketing Sales Operations	Number of inquiries Cost per Inquiry
Fulfill Product Orders (Order to cash)	Orders	Record Pick, Pack Ship Invoice Collect	Cash	Sales Call Center Operations Procurement Finance	DSO % not perfect
Fulfill Service Orders	Inquiries Orders	Record Quote Schedule Deliver	Cash	Sales Call Center Finance	DSO % not perfect
Develop Services	Growth strategies Budgets	Idea generation Feasibility Analysis Development Testing Launch	Orders	Consulting Marketing Finance Sales	Number of Orders % Revenue - New
Procure	Forecasts Usage	Analyze Place orders Receive product Pay suppliers	Product	Procurement Operations Finance	Asset Utilization % product orders not perfect
Deploy Technology	Operational requirements Budgets	Monitor Assess Define Develop Implement Operate	Current and new functionality	IT All others	% downtime $ value created
Report Financial Performance	Strategy Budgets Actuals	Gather data Analyze variances Prepare reports	Financial statements	Finance All others	Accuracy Timeliness

Table 3.3. Sample Working Document - The Enterprise View

There are three significant benefits to preparing such a working document. First, it clarifies the proposed process definitions. Next, since the departments that participate in each process are listed, it raises awareness of the need for cross-departmental collaboration. Then, it potentially raises cross-process dependency issues.

Of course, the development of such a plan needs to begin with an objective assessment of the size of the gap between current performance and desired performance. One might surmise that the best way to do this is to translate the firm's strategic objectives into business process terms. But there is frequently a problem with that approach. Many firms do not have clear, actionable strategies because of the way in which the firm's strategy has been developed. They never considered what it means to frame strategic objectives in terms of end-to-end activities.

The transition from expressing strategy in general terms or in broad financial terms to expressing strategy in terms of observable activity terms requires both careful thought and a shift in mindset. Only when a leadership team begins to believe that a customer centric, activity based approach leads to greater leverage of the organization's capability can this framework be fully developed.

The shift in mindset involves a deep appreciation that the financial goals are simply the cumulative outcomes of the activities that the firm executes. Careful thought is necessary to make tough choices on the deployment of limited resources.

It is important then to appreciate the following factors, which underlie these decisions:

- a shared understanding of the definition of each enterprise level business process, including details on where the process starts, where it ends, the key steps, and a high level view of the departments involved
- clarity and agreement on the critical few measures of performance for each process
- acceptance of the estimates of current performance for each process
- agreement on the size of the performance gap that needs to be bridged

- agreement on the top priorities for improvement, allocation of resources, and deep dedication to taking action
- a shared understanding of accountability assignments, in other words, who shall be accountable for the improvement and management of the company's enterprise-level business processes.

Table 3.4 illustrates a sample process improvement that outlines on a single page the key components of a management plan for a hypothetical mortgage services company.

Plans cannot be translated into action without a clear, shared understanding of the accountability for improving and managing the firm's major enterprise level business processes. In most firms, no one person has authority or control over the entire set of activities in an end-to-end business process, although it is often possible to identify readily the person who has the greatest amount of "skin in the game" of the desired outcomes. Accordingly, the role of the process owner at the enterprise level is central to any company wide effort in performing for customers.

The accountability for the ownership of the organization's critical processes involves a multifaceted role and is instrumental in:

- Promoting a shift from "traditional" thinking
- Enabling cross regional, cross-functional, and cross-business unit collaboration
- Facilitating a focused effort on performance planning and management
- Reinforcing the focus on process measures – "what gets measured – gets done"

The crucial role of process ownership or stewardship was emphasized by Steve Stanton in the April 2005 edition of BP Trends. Stanton defined the principal activities of process owners as involving advocacy, boundary management, collaboration, improvement, and metrics.[4]

Accountability for the performance of a company's critical business processes is the glue that binds corporate performance to customer requirements. There is no one best practice in terms of defining the accountability for improving and managing a company's business processes. In some organizations, key executives wear two hats, one for their business or functional responsibility and another for monitoring, improving, and managing the performance of an enterprise level business process. Alternatively, some companies have elected to appoint dedicated process owners. In both cases, it is only partly tongue in cheek to say that the three critical success factors of process ownership are "influence, influence, and influence."[5]

Business Process	Output	Measures	Performance Gap	Process Owner	Likely Action
Promote	Inquiries	Number of inquiries Cost per inquiry	Cost per inquiry is too high	VP Marketing	Improve
Sell	Completed Mortgage Applications	% conversion Revenue Accuracy Completeness Timeliness	% conversion from inquiry to completed application too low	VP Sales	Improve
Mortgage Processing	Closing and funded loans	On time Complete & accurate Cost per unit Customer Satisfaction	Cost per unit too high, maybe by as much as 20%	VP Operations	Redesign
Mortgage Administration		Per unit cost # errors	Per unit cost slightly above target	VP Administration	Manage
Develop Technology	Existing and new functionality	Downtime Help desk responsiveness Value added	Need new applications to reduce cost per unit of mortgage processing	CIO	Improve

Table 3.4. Sample Process Improvement and Management Plan

Exercising influence is certainly one of the critical success factors in the improvement and management of end-to-end business processes. The ability to influence peers, who are often remote either functionally or geographically, is an essential skill set for process managers at all levels and particularly for process owners. This has everything to do with the fact that the enterprise level processes are simply too large for any one individual to have overall control. The well thought-out exercise of influence therefore becomes a critical skill set.

In *Influence without Authority,* the authors provide valuable guidance on this topic that's of particular use to process owners. Their model, depicted in Figure 3.3 below, is based in part on being clear about your goals, understanding others' points of view, seeking out viable options, and understanding the big picture and the principles of fair exchange.[6]

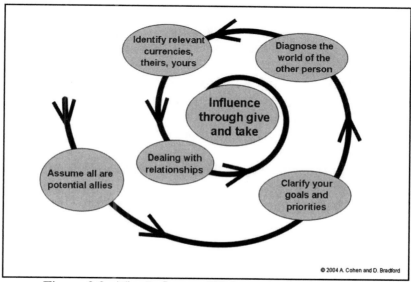

Figure 3.3. The Influence Without Authority Model

It would be difficult to overemphasize the centrality of influencing skills in process management success. It applies equally to the role of process owner or steward and the role of middle managers involved on a process improvement team. In both cases, the ability for one individual to influence another depends directly on understanding the big picture, being clear about goals, understanding other people's points of view, and collaboratively seeking out viable options.

Building the ability to collaborate is why many firms find that making the transition from a traditional view to a process view takes considerable time, effort, and commitment. This is particularly true in the case of global firms where regional differences also need to be addressed.

Dave Burritt, at Caterpillar Inc., described what is needed to champion the ownership of major cross-functional processes when the effort needs to occur on *global basis,* as follows:

> You've got to be prepared to take a few bullets. When you rollout global processes, you touch other units' stuff. As soon as you touch their stuff, they tend to push back. They would rather keep control themselves. That's why you need a strong global process owner and a good team. It's not a case of "if you build it, they will come." You can't just put a global process in place and expect everyone to adopt it. You need to support the process with the right organizational design, including a robust set of metrics that captures the "truth" about the value the process creates for the stock-holders.

> Few companies take a "big bang" approach where they rollout all their global processes at once. That approach overwhelms an enterprise. You end up with global process cheerleaders, not true global process owners. We have an adaptive strategy and are selecting a few global processes that will drive enterprise value. We are picking the essential few processes and putting the right people in place to drive them.

Assuming that the elements outlined above are in place, the final component in this planning stage is a solid communication plan that both engages people in the organization and moves people to action. The importance of such a communication plan is clear to the leaders of high performing companies. When Michael Dell and Kevin Rollins were asked how they implanted the famous Dell execution-oriented DNA in their company, their answer was, "We drummed into our people's heads, in presentation after presentation, what's good performance and what's bad performance."[7]

Therefore, a superior communication plan needs to deploy various media, including, but not limited to, town hall meetings, broadcast email, presentations, and even video clips – exploiting communications that go beyond standard presentations in order to impress with the need for innovative action.

As if the above benefits of process thinking with respect to achieving clarity on strategic direction weren't enough, a process view of the enterprise is also instrumental in avoiding initiative overload.

Initiative overload occurs when a firm launches more change initiatives than can be reasonably expected to be executed. Sadly, this is observed all too frequently. Most often, it is the result of strategy being defined in functional terms, and department heads having the license to launch as many independent, uncoordinated initiatives as their budgets will permit.

In *Change without Pain*, Eric Abrahamson coined the phrase "repetitive change syndrome." He contends that the symptoms of "repetitive change syndrome" include both initiative overload and change related chaos leading to widespread cynicism and other related symptoms that make organizational change harder to manage, more expensive to implement, and more likely to fail.[8]

Process thinking can be a powerful force in militating against initiative overload, as long as the firm applies it in a systemic way. That requires a plan and a set of priorities which clearly answer the question, "Which of our core processes need to be improved by how much – by when – in order to achieve our strategic goals?" Then it becomes a matter of exercising the needed discipline to focus on the top priority cross-functional projects.

That said, there's a lot more involved in achieving sustainable, superior performance than process thinking. As Michael Treacy said when asked what organizations should do in terms of implementing strategy, "What I'm most concerned about is winning, and a piece of that may have to do with process – but only a piece." For Treacy the other pieces are talent, information, and management routine. That's probably true, but how to get leaders to better understand that customer centric, process thinking is a part of "winning," and an important one at that, is the challenge. And the primary obstacle in this respect is the traditional, functional mindset of many executives and managers.

You will appreciate that the framework for action discussed above is simply a plan for improving a company's high level processes, albeit, an important one. Yet, it's one that relatively few organizations take the time to develop. The fundamental management practice involved in this respect is outlined in Table 3.5 below.[9]

What's Needed	What's Involved
An enterprise view or schematic and a plan on performing for customers	▪ Measure what counts to customers ▪ Define the set of enterprise business processes ▪ Build a process management plan that bridges performance gaps such that goals will be met ▪ Build and deploy a communication plan on which processes need to be improved by how much for the firm to achieve its goals

Table 3.5. The Enterprise Process View

This chapter has addressed measuring what counts to customers, articulating strategy in a process context with clarity on accountability and the need to broadly communicate the plan. Other principles will be addressed in later chapters.

The companies who have progressed in the deployment of process orientation at the leadership level typically share certain significant characteristics and appear to place value on enabling leadership mindset and behavior. They recognize the importance of collaboration across departments and geographies. Since most enterprise business processes are simply too large to be under the direct control of any one executive, successful leaders emphasize the development of their skills in influencing their peers.

The way in which companies behaved in developing these characteristics can vary somewhat. But there is a recipe that can be followed to develop a meaningful enterprise view. If your organization dedicates the needed time and energy to develop an enterprise view of how value is created, you can expect the following benefits:

- Clarity on what matters most to customers and the critical few measures that define performance
- A more unified leadership team with consensus on a plan for improving and managing enterprise level business processes
- A keener sense for cross-department interdependence and clarity around accountability for results
- A communication plan that inspires and moves people to action

Table 3.6 illustrates some of the key signs of progress.

What's Needed	Signs of Progress
An enterprise view or schematic and a plan on performing for customers	• Your people are clear on what matters to customers • The high level enterprise schematic is prominently displayed and understood • Process owners of your firm's critical business processes visibly accept and highlight their role • Your people are clear on which business processes are most in need of improvement and why • Leaders relentlessly communicate on the central role of improving and managing business processes

Table 3.6. Signs of Progress

Like any recipe, the proof is in the tasting. The quality of the ingredients and the chef's skill does matter enormously. The consumers, in this case, are customers and employees. They will decide.

In order to deliver "more for less," a company's process management plan needs to be implemented. That requires clarity on the key components of the plan: process definition, clear accountability, the size of the performance gap to be closed, the key metrics, and the relative priority for improvement. It will also involve a more granular view of a company's business processes, with a focus on the cross-functional collaboration needed to perform for customers, which in turn entails even more new ways of thinking about the business.

Chapter 3: Self-Assessment Questions

1. To what extent does the leadership team see the business from the outside-in as well as the inside-out?
2. What picture dominates the thinking of your leadership team – the organization chart or a process view of the business?
3. Have you developed a core strategy that is tightly integrated with the definition, management, and improvement of the enterprise's business processes?
4. Is there a shared understanding as to which of your business processes need to be improved and by how much in order to achieve your strategic objectives?
5. Have you undertaken a deliberate effort to articulate and communicate the firm's strategy such that it inspires people and remains front and center throughout the year?
6. Have you documented and communicated the links/interdependencies among the critical enterprise processes?
7. Is the enterprise-wide performance measurement system "hard-wired" to budgets and operating reviews?
8. How well have you expressed both the financial and non-financial business process goals that define the strategic success of your enterprise?
9. How fluid is the top-down and bottom-up flow of information on progress towards achieving your strategic objectives?
10. Have you assured that each department's roles and incentives reflect the contributions it needs to make to improve the performance of critical enterprise business processes?
11. Is your firm suffering from too many disconnected projects, initiative overload, or "repetitive change syndrome?"

References.

[1] McCormack, Kevin, 'Business Process Orientation: Do You Have It?', *Quality Progress*, January 2001

[2] Rummler, Geary A. and Alan Brache, *Improving Performance: How to Manage the White Space on the Organization Chart*, Jossey-Bass, 1995.

[3] Provided by George Maszle, Xerox Corporation

[4] Stanton, Steve, 'So What Does a Process Owner Really Do?', *BP Trends*, April 2005

[5] Hammer, Michael and Steven Stanton, 'How Process Enterprises Really Work,' *Harvard Business Review*, November - December 1999.

[6] Cohen, Allan and David Bradford, *Influence without Authority*, 2nd edition, *Wiley*, 2005

[7] 'Execution without Excuses: The HBR Interview', *Harvard Business Review*, March 2005

[8] Abrahamson, Eric, *Change Without Pain*, Harvard Business School Press, 2004

[9] Spanyi, Andrew, *Business Process Management is a Team Sport*, Anclote Press, 2003. Note that the management practices cited above are adapted from the principles outlined in this reference.

Four

Process Design:
From Planning to Action

I have been impressed with the urgency of doing. Knowing is not enough; we must apply. Being willing is not enough; we must do.
– Leonardo da Vinci

It's easy to forget that the principal reason to improve a company's business processes is to create more value for customers and shareholders. The enterprise level plan provides the needed focus and set of priorities. It is an essential prerequisite for performance improvement, but it is just a plan. To improve performance you must convert plans into action through the improvement and management of the corporation's critical business processes.

This involves process improvement initiatives or projects. In fact, demonstrated results from the successful implementation of process improvements can do more to shift mindset and culture than even the best management rhetoric.

To improve a company's large business processes requires the type of collaboration not commonly observed in traditional organizations. While a sound, replicable, and efficient method of improvement is essential, leadership mindset and behavior are arguably even more important.

As a leader, you may not need to know the intricate details and tools of various improvement methods, but you should certainly understand the key phases of the methods in use within your organization and the role of the leader in each phase.

Now, you may be thinking that a lot has been written about the mechanics of process improvement methods. You'd be right. However, far less attention has been dedicated to the leadership attitude and aptitude required for successful improvement of a company's enterprise processes.

Over time there have been various approaches to improving and redesigning business processes. Many methods for process improvement contain elements similar to those depicted in Table 4.1 below.

Harrington[1]	Davenport[2]	Hammer[3]	Six Sigma[4]
▪ Organization	▪ Select processes	▪ Scoping	▪ Define
▪ Documentation	▪ Identify Change Enabler	▪ Organizing	▪ Measure
▪ Analysis	▪ Develop Business Vision and Process Objectives	▪ Redesigning	▪ Analyze
▪ Design	▪ Understand and Improve Existing Processes	▪ Implementing	▪ Improve
▪ Implementation	▪ Design the New Process & Organization		▪ Control
▪ Management	▪ Implement the New Process-Based Organization		

Table 4.1. Various Methods of Process Improvement

While there are important nuances and subtleties in the differences among these approaches to process improvement, most methods for improving business processes involve the following basic activities. Once the process or processes for improvement have been selected, the first step is to scope or further define the initiative; then, analyze current business practices; then, design future business practices; then, implement the design; and, finally, manage or control for continuous improvement.

In this generic model the key phases or stages of process improvement are Definition, Analysis, Design, Implementation, and Management.[5]

Do you understand the discrete activities in each of these phases? Do you know the salient aspects of leadership mindset and behavior involved in each phase or stage of an improvement project? If not, consider the practical guidance in what follows. You will note that leadership mindset and behavior is what makes the difference between firms who excel at process improvement and those who don't, as outlined below.

Definition

Defining a process improvement project generally includes an agreement on process boundaries, goals/objectives, participants, constraints, and schedule.

The leaders of firms that excel at executing the improvement of large cross-functional business processes understand that the rapid yet thorough definition of the project is a fundamental and critical success factor.

Outlined below are the key leadership perspectives and behaviors involved in the definition of process improvement projects.

Mindset	Behavior
▪ Customer centric view ▪ Focus on clarity ▪ Strive for shared understanding ▪ Look for and address early signs of resistance	▪ Agree on process boundaries ▪ Set clear improvement goals ▪ Appoint the best people ▪ Identify realistic constraints ▪ Set a clear schedule ▪ Charter to implement, not just to design

Table 4.2. Definition Phase

Achieving clarity and a shared understanding of process boundaries are essential. In most cases, this means clearly identifying the inputs, key steps, outputs, key metrics, and a first draft estimate of current performance for the process under consideration. A customer centric view in this activity is vital, where the following key questions are asked and answered: Who is the customer? What do they receive? What level of performance is expected? How are we doing now? How well do we wish to do? Where does the process start? What are the key steps? Where does it end? What's in/what's out of scope as far as this project is concerned?

Leaders of firms adept at improving large, cross-functional processes realize the importance of having specific goals andobjectives that clearly answer the question: What do we want to accomplish by when? A couple of examples of such specific goals and objectives are:

- Improve the on-time, defect free performance of our order fulfillment process from 78% to 95% within 12 months, while reducing process costs by 20%.
- Improve the firm's ability to introduce product revisions and enhancements by reducing the average cycle time by 30% within the next 12 months.

Note how these goals differ from broad general statements such as "Improve order fulfillment performance" or "Gain clarity on roles and responsibilities in the product." While there is nothing wrong with making general statements, they do not provide sufficient specific guidance for improvement projects.

Øystein Risan, the Operations Director for NSB, a national railway company, emphasized the importance and the difficulty of linking business process to the overall business objectives. He said,

I think linking everything to the overall business objectives – what the customer wants – to find a way to measure and follow up on everything we do – that's become a much bigger challenge than I thought initially. So we spend a lot of effort on that. Why? I think generally people become very inward looking and focused on internal life – especially in big organizations, and that's a big mental challenge to change.

Some firms have developed increasing skill in translating project benefits to financial metrics. At Xerox, the assessment of project potential and of success goes beyond simple cost reduction or revenue enhancement to a metric called "economic profit," which is defined as the "income generated relative to all resources required including capital costs."[6] Linking project success to factors such as "economic profit" is most useful with respect to projects involving the improvement of large business processes, but can also be usefully applied to projects of smaller scope.

Involving the right people at the right level is another key discipline practiced by leaders at successful firms. This includes having clear leadership and accountability for the results of the process improvement project in the form of a project champion or owner and in having the right mix of representation on both the management team and the working team from key departments that are touched by the process.

Establishing clear and reasonable constraints on the project is an additional discipline in the definition phase. This constitutes developing specific statements on any limitations to be imposed on the project. Typical examples include information systems that cannot be touched, organization changes that cannot be recommended, and restrictions on access to funding or specific ROI that must be met. Not only should these constraints be clearly stated, it is equally important that the constraints do not unfairly hinder the attainment of project goals.

A further discipline practiced by leaders of successful firms in the definition phase of a major process improvement project is the establishment of a clear schedule – including key meeting dates and milestones – that extends through the analysis phase to the end of the design phase. Further, while it may be impractical physically to schedule meetings beyond a certain point, firms that are adept at process improvement will task the working team with responsibility to implement – not just to design. They understand the importance of having continuity of team members beyond design through to implementation.

What are some of the major pitfalls to avoid in the definition phase?

You will appreciate that if the above represents desirable disciplines and behaviors in developing the definition of a process improvement project, then the opposite of each should be avoided. So it is important to avoid a failure to achieve clarity and a shared understanding of process boundaries. Avoid not having specific goals and objectives; avoid a failure to take accountability for the project; avoid vacillation on key decisions; and avoid failure to establish clear and reasonable constraints; and so on. Other pitfalls for leaders to avoid in the definition phase include the following.

Failing to capture specific current performance data – even if it is just by way of random sampling during the definition phase is a major pitfall to avoid. The typical excuse is "This will take too long – we can do this later– during the analysis phase." But the fact is that development of so-called SMART goals (specific, measurable, attainable, realistic, tangible) relies upon a sense for the level of current performance. This data gathering does not need to be time consuming. The judicious use of the 80/20 rule generally facilitates getting some reasonable estimate in weeks versus months.

Not involving the right people on the project Steering Team is another frequently observed pitfall. With some process improvement approaches, this involves over-reliance on the project champion, and insufficient appreciation for the fact that the improvement of large cross-functional processes demands cross-functional collaboration at both management and operational levels. At the management level, this mostly has to do with the selection of Steering Team members. But the selection of the Design Team members is equally vital.

A related oversight is the failure to address silent dissent. This occurs when someone is clearly thinking, "You guys go ahead as long as it doesn't affect my department." This type of behavior needs to be nipped in the bud if the project is to have a reasonable chance of success.

Failure to provide training in a common improvement methodology on a timely basis for both Steering Team and Design Team members is something else to avoid. Assuming that everything will be fine as long as people have been trained in some process improvement methodology during the past few years is a big mistake. It can have serious consequences since the half-life of training is pretty short, and vocabulary matters enormously when it comes to the analysis and design of large processes.

Then there's the failure to set a project schedule appropriate to the targeted scope of improvement. Many executives do not appreciate that it is the planned scope of improvement, or the size of the performance gap that needs to be closed, that is the major driver of the resource intensity needed for the project. To achieve an ambitious improvement in process performance of a complex cross-functional process – say, around 30-50% – in relatively short order, invariably calls for the use of a full time team. The most commonly observed pitfall is the deployment of a part-time team, with a meeting schedule that involves one half day per week, or less, to tackle an ambitious improvement goal for a complex cross-functional process.

Xerox is one company that appears to be aware of the importance of selecting the right projects. Figure 4.1 depicts the Xerox approach to project selection.

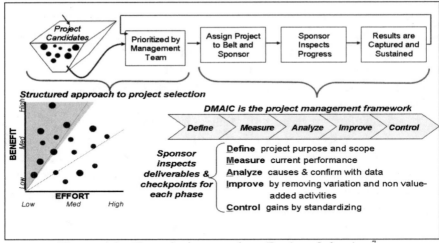

Figure 4.1. Xerox's Approach to Project Selection[7]

Xerox has standardized on the use of the Lean Six Sigma method of process improvement. It appears to have achieved some insight on the key point that customer issues and opportunities and business results are what drive project selection. It has applied a structured approach to project selection based in part on mapping the location of projects on a grid of potential economic benefit versus the anticipated degree of effort required.

Analysis

The analysis of a large, complex, cross-functional process generally includes the following typical components: development of a cross-functional process map which describes the current state (often called the "As Is"), further development and analysis of process performance measures, identification of problems, issues or disconnects which adversely impact the performance of the process, assessment of the impact of these issues, and their relative priority.

Leaders of firms that excel at executing the improvement of large cross-functional business processes understand that the rapid yet thorough analysis of the process is a fundamental and critical success factor. This is predicated on the belief that the principal benefits of analyzing the current state, or the "As Is," are related to the development of a shared understanding by both the Steering Team and the Design Team on how work is done today. There is an inverse relationship between the targeted scope of change and the amount of time spent on analysis. The less ambitious the scope of change, the more time spent on analysis. The more ambitious the scope of change, the less time spent on analysis.

Why is that? Incremental improvement projects focus on a series of small changes to an existing design, while projects, which target radical improvement, will likely challenge the fundamentals of current business practice in introducing quantum change. Yet, a rapid assessment of the current state can be instrumental in creating a base of common understanding for the development of even a breakthrough design, and later on it can be useful in establish a starting point from which implementation of the eventual design will be launched.

The key leadership mindset and behaviors practiced by leaders of firms adept at process analysis are outlined below.

Mindset	Behavior
■ Customer centric view ■ Focus on rapid, thorough analysis ■ Discipline in impact analysis	■ Understand the flow of work in a cross-functional context ■ Agree on the level of current performance and the size of the performance gap ■ Gain clarity on key issues, disconnects, opportunities ■ Insist on the prioritization of issues based on impact ■ Refine working team membership based on the insights at the end of this phase, if necessary

Table 4.3. Analysis Phase

The leaders of firms that have become adept at process analysis recognize the value of rapidly developing the cross-functional process map. They have found that the development of a draft cross-functional "As Is" map in "swim lane" format enables the working team or Design Team to do their work more effectively in this phase as it visually depicts the handoffs in the process and emphasizes the need for cross-group collaboration. Since the draft map needs to be refined by the Design Team in order to gain a shared understanding of how the entire process currently works, an 80% correct draft map is normally sufficient. The development of a draft "As Is" cross-functional process map is best accomplished through facilitation as opposed to prescription. This is often accomplished by conducting a series of interviews with Design Team members and others who are familiar with their part of the process in advance of convening a team session, such that there is a "draft" document. Then, the task of the Design Team group workshop is to refine a draft document in a team meeting and focus on the identification and impact or issues and opportunities. When this approach is followed, Design Team members often remark, "This is the first time I've seen how the whole thing works end-to-end." Of equal importance is that this approach begins building a momentum for change at the grass roots level.

Another practice common to firms who have become adept at analyzing the performance of large cross-functional processes is to develop increased confidence and clarity on the level of current performance and the size of the performance gap. This generally involves the use of statistical tools to better understand the variability in performance in terms of time, quality, and cost.

Arguably, one of the most important aspects of the analysis phase is the identification and impact assessment of disconnects, issues, or problems within the process. Some firms prefer to view these problems from a positive perspective and frame them as "opportunities for improvement." These are really two sides of the same coin.

Just consider this example. A typical problem in the order fulfillment process is duplicate data entry. Firms that elect to view problems as disconnects will identify the frequency of duplicate data entry, and its resource intensity, and will assess the impact accordingly. Firms that elect to view problems as opportunities will also identify the frequency of duplicate data entry and their resource intensity, and they will represent the impact of eliminating this problem as an opportunity for improvement.

Leaders of firms that have become proficient at analyzing the performance of complex, cross-functional processes recognize the importance of the dialogue between the Design Team and the Steering Team. They will typically schedule a session for this dialogue and will take the time to review the cross-functional "As Is" map, current performance measures, and the relevant top priority disconnects (or opportunities for improvement) in order to assure that there is a shared understanding of the level of current performance. In most cases, this dialogue will lead to certain insights into issues such as the extent of IT involvement needed in the design phase and to other insights on the likely direction of the design.

This dialogue may also lead to the recognition that some realignment of Design Team membership may be in order. Firms experienced in process improvement appreciate that the skill sets for designing a new process are not necessarily the same as those needed to analyze the performance of a current process. So some additions or changes to the Design Team's members are sometimes valuable. When this occurs, the leaders understand that it is essential to orient new members through training in a common method of process improvement and conduct a review of the work that has already taken place.

It is also useful to be aware of some of the major pitfalls to avoid in the analysis phase.

These include, but are not limited to, taking too long for analysis, failure to pay close attention to cross-functional handoffs, and not being specific enough.

Taking too long in the analysis phase for complex, cross-functional processes is one of the most common pitfalls. In most instances, it is sufficient to document the process at the activity level and not drill down to the task level. When a firm has a history of improving processes within a given function or department – where prior practice involved the detailed analysis at the task level – it may be difficult to break this habit in addressing cross-functional, end-to-end processes. Yet this can lead to a great deal of wasted time and effort and dilute the focus on what really matters in the end-to-end view.

A related pitfall is the failure to pay close attention to cross-functional handoffs. This can be a significant oversight, for the location of cross-functional handoffs is where some of most significant opportunities for improvement are frequently found.

One of the most common and severe pitfalls to avoid is not being specific enough in terms of the major disconnects that currently adversely impact performance (or the opportunities for improvement which exist). This often occurs where too much attention is dedicated to the details of process activity, and not enough to the intelligent analysis of the activity flow.

Thoughtful leaders understand that the true value of the analysis phase is mostly about just that – disciplined analysis. They understand that engaging employees in disciplined analysis begins to build the case for change at the grass roots level.

Design

While there are a number of different approaches to developing a new design for a single, cross-functional process, leaders should look for certain aspects of any new design. These include the following:

- a concise, compelling vision for the new design
- a cross-functional process map of the way in which business should be conducted in the future to achieve goals
- a clear matrix of performance measures that should be monitored in the future
- a concise set of recommendations for change to achieve stated goals
- a document which details changes in roles and accountabilities such that there is clarity on who needs to do what in the new process
- a compelling business case
- a high level implementation plan that indicates who will need to do what by when to install new business practices, process changes, and related technology, with approximate milestones

The above points are not meant to be all-inclusive. Instead, they represent the minimum requirements for a comprehensive design. Leaders of firms that excel at executing the improvement of large cross-functional business processes understand that the bulk of the effort should be dedicated to the creative, yet thorough, design of the new process. This is not limited purely to process or workflow considerations alone. Instead, the new design needs to encompass needed changes in performance measurement, enabling technology, changes in roles, accountabilities, and other pertinent factors.

Again, the development of a shared understanding by both the Steering Team and the Design Team on how work will be done in the future, and the path to get there is essential.

The principal aspects of leadership mindset and behaviors practiced by leaders of firms adept at process design are outlined below.

Mindset	Behavior
▪ Maintain focus on the customer centric view	▪ Probe to test the vision for the new design
▪ Emphasize the value of continuing dialogue	▪ Understand the cross-functional implications of how business should be conducted in the future
▪ Embrace a shared vision	
▪ Insist on concise metrics, recommendations and roadmap	▪ Gain clarity on the matrix of performance measures
▪ Look for and address emerging signs of resistance	▪ Constructively challenge the set of recommendations for change
▪ Take the time to do it right	▪ Assess the business case
▪ Pay attention to the degree of organizational readiness for change	▪ Inspect the high level implementation plan

Table 4.4. Design Phase

Firms that are adept at designing the improvement of large cross-functional business processes have leaders who understand the importance of a concise, compelling vision supported by a short list of desirable characteristics that the new process needs to incorporate.

The development of a concise, compelling vision, supported by process characteristics, also assists in calibrating the innovativeness of the design effort to the contemplated scope of improvement.

Thoughtful leaders also recognize that improving the performance of large processes is not just about process. So they expect to see a set of integrated recommendations for change, which invariably will include the deployment of enabling technology, training, performance measurement, and may also include changes to compensation, geographic location, etc. Since the use of information technology is so central to most improvement efforts, these firms pay close attention to the collaborative role played by representatives from the firm's information systems department in analysis, design, and implementation. They ensure that IT is well represented on both the Design Team and the Steering Team, and pay particular attention to the level of IT commitment to the proposed priority of IT support and to see that needed resources are made available.

These leaders also appreciate that continuing dialogue between the Steering Team and Design Team, on a periodic basis, is another important feature of successful process improvement projects. This dialogue has dual benefits. First, it is an essential mechanism to maintain momentum and engagement. But it also provides a forum to spot potential roadblocks and obstacles to the eventual implementation of the design. Prompt, decisive action by the project sponsor or champion in addressing such potential roadblocks and obstacles is a critical success factor in this respect.

The close connection between the business case and a high level implementation plan is an equally important element in successful projects. In this regard, the insight on the real return on investment in implementing the proposed design detailed in the business case is supported by estimates of the resource intensity and timing of the implementation, with estimates of who needs to do what by when for success.

The following are some of more typical pitfalls encountered in the design phase.

Incomplete recommendations for change represent a serious weakness in the design phase. A couple of examples of such incomplete recommendations are "Define functional roles and accountabilities aligned with process objectives" and "Identify and implement a CRM system to enable process performance." There are two principal drawbacks to such incomplete recommendations for change statements. First, they push work that genuinely belongs in the design phase into the implementation phase and thereby compromise the accuracy of resources needed for implementation. Also, they do not provide clarity on the scope of change and, in so doing, risk failing to surface potential objections to the design. The development of an effective design involves balance. Sufficient details are essential for the purpose of developing the business case and realistic estimates of implementation. On the other hand, it is important to avoid delving into such minute detail that the time required to complete the design compromises needed momentum and engagement.

Failure to test the design against the major issues or disconnects uncovered in the analysis phase represents another serious pitfall. This is particularly important in those projects where the goal is an incremental improvement in the 10% range, as such levels of improvement can often be achieved by simply eliminating the adverse impact of the major issues. Using the list of major issues or disconnects uncovered in the analysis phase to test an innovative, breakthrough design is also effective.

Failure to test certain aspects of organizational readiness for change is another potential problem in the design phase. This is particularly important when some aspect of the design requires a functional area to dedicate resources to implement a key aspect of the design in such a way that may be incompatible with that department's current list of priorities. Failure to take the time and effort offline to test the level of readiness of such key departments leads to obstacles in obtaining approval to implement the design and needless frustration later on in the implementation phase.

Implementation

The implementation of a cross-functional design is much like any large complex project and has the same inherent risks and challenges. As the June 11, 2005, edition of *The Economist* reported, in their article "Project Management," there is scant evidence that companies are getting any better at implementing large, complex projects. This is particularly true of information systems projects, where The Standish Group estimated that in 2004 only 29% of IT projects were on time and on budget, and that is down from 34% in 2002.[8]

There are at least seven business practices employed by firms adept in implementing complex, cross-functional process designs. These are outlined in "The Seven Cs of Implementation:"

1. Common Goal and Measures
2. Cross-functional Commitment
3. Continuity
4. Clear Communication
5. Competent Project Management
6. Credible Coaching
7. Celebration

The effective implementation of a complex process design is characterized by focus on common goals and measures. In most instances, especially when implementing designs that have to do with customer touching processes, this involves clarity on the set of customer benefits and company benefits to be achieved. Project goals and benefits need to be positioned center stage throughout the implementation process, and regularly supported by the entire executive team. The role of measures is critical and extends beyond implementation to the ongoing management of the process.

Successful implementation efforts also call for deep cross-functional commitment. This is manifested initially by dedicating significantly more resources to implementation than was needed for the design phase. It is not unusual to see implementation teams that are two to four times as large in number as the Design Team. The needed level of commitment is characterized not only by making skilled resources available, but also by taking the time and effort necessary to orient the new members of the Implementation Team properly to the history and rationale underpinning the design. This is worth the time investment as the larger number of resources committed during implementation also serves ensure a broader base of buy-in and responsibility for the new process once implemented.

Another important facet is assuring a high level of continuity from the Design Team to the implementation effort, which is necessary to assure the integrity of the design throughout implementation. Continuity of regular dialogue between the leaders of the Steering Team and the Implementation Team is yet another distinctive attribute of the level of leadership commitment needed for successful implementation efforts characterized by broad cross-functional collaboration and cooperation. The importance of continuity extends beyond the implementation phase to the ongoing management of the process. Accordingly, setting up the appropriate infrastructure for the ongoing monitoring of process performance and its continuous improvement is necessary for the sustainability of the results.

Clear communication of project goals and milestones to stakeholders impacted by the effort is equally essential. This is not only needed in the early phases of implementation, but is equally critical on a continuing basis, especially as key milestones are reached. The clarity of communication needs to be matched by consistency in delivery by various executives in their interaction with key players in their departments.

Competent project management practices are arguably one of the more crucial aspects in the effective implementation of a complex process design. Well-crafted work breakdown structures, clear responsibility assignments, milestone reviews, and robust risk management are some of the needed elements. The cross-functional interaction intrinsic to many such implementation efforts demands the discipline that project management practices offer.

Credible coaching is a characteristic of successful implementation efforts at several levels. The importance of credible coaching is most visible in the interaction of Steering Team members with the Implementation Team leaders when addressing roadblocks and obstacles in new process implementation. It is of similar importance in terms of the interaction between the Implementation Team leaders and individual contributors.

Celebration of accomplishments is the last, but certainly not the least, of the Seven Cs. Most successful implementation efforts are planned to yield benefits early in the cycle. Often called "early wins" or "quick wins," each of these efforts represents an opportunity for celebration, which helps maintain enthusiasm and the momentum needed to face up to the challenges in the latter stages of implementation. An ongoing program of celebration is particularly beneficial in those projects that need to be phased due to inherent complexity.

By now, you may be asking yourself, what about change management? Isn't change management one of the critical success factors of successfully implementing large projects? Of course, it is. But consider this. Change management is actually the effective execution of the entire set of the Seven Cs: Common Goal and Measures, Cross-functional Commitment, Continuity, Clear Communication, Competent Project Management, Credible Coaching, and Celebration.

What are some of the major pitfalls to avoid in the implementation phase of large process improvement projects?

These include, but are no means limited to, not establishing a sufficient sense of urgency, failing to assess organizational readiness for change, not planning systematically for so-called "quick wins," and not acting promptly and decisively to remove obstacles to the new way of working.

Failing to establish a sufficient sense of urgency can be fatal since the implementation of large improvement projects relies largely on momentum. All too often, leaders expend all of their energy in the earlier phases of the project and have little "oomph" left for the really hard work of implementation. Then, there's the executive phenomenon of believing that once something is designed and agreed upon —it's as good as done. Little could be further from the truth. That's why deep cross-functional commitment and constant communication are so essential. In the absence of a sense of urgency, other priorities will intrude and disrupt the needed focus.

Failing to plan systematically for so-called "quick wins" basically means that there won't be much to celebrate in the early stages of the project. Momentum suffers in the absence of early success.

Failing to take the effort to assess rapidly the degree of organizational readiness for change is almost like asking for adversity. Otherwise, how will you know where, and who, might represent major obstacles and roadblocks to the implementation effort?

Closely related to the failure of assessing the degree of organizational readiness for change is not acting promptly and decisively to remove obstacles to the new way of working. Not everyone will buy-in to major change. Those who don't — need to be moved or removed. As Jack Welch related with respect to his change efforts at G.E., "My main job was developing talent. I was a gardener providing water and other nourishment to our top 750 people. Of course, I had to pull out some weeds, too."[9]

In this respect, shifting priorities for the needed level of IT support is one of the more commonly observed and serious obstacles that need to be addressed head on.

Management

The ongoing management of the improved process is at least as problematic as the implementation of a large process improvement project. That's because the ongoing management of an improved process is what drives the sustainability of the improvement and requires a longer-term shift in executive mindset and behavior.

The fundamental requirements for the ongoing management of a large cross-functional process are:

- An agreed upon set of performance metrics to be used in monitoring process performance
- A designated process owner or steward who is accountable for the performance of the process and therefore continuously monitors and takes action to improve it
- A standing cross-functional process team which acts to continuously improve the performance of the process
- Clear accountability for process/sub-process performance
- A standing program for executive and management training on the selected approach to process improvement
- Visible and meaningful incentives to work cross-functionally

The core concept in the ongoing management of a business process is accountability for performance. The challenge is that when it comes to any large, cross-functional process, no one executive can possibly control all the resources attached to that process. That's why a change in the traditional mindset is an absolute prerequisite for success, not only in terms of the mindset of the individual who is charged with the ownership or stewardship of the process, but also in terms of the mindset and behaviors of the other department heads who have a stake in that process' performance.

Sustainable success in the management of a large cross-functional process is essentially about customer centricity and leadership. That is why a change of personnel, especially at the top, is the single largest threat to continuous improvement through ongoing process management. As might be expected, changes in key personnel invariably involve questioning what prior management had done. In some cases, the principal reason to discard a previous management practice is no more complex than that it was not initiated by the person currently in office.

The most effective defense against the threat of a change in personnel is to embed the principles of customer centricity and process focus in the culture of the organization. The concept of imbedding process centricity into an organization via its culture is vital, and it has to be more than merely stating it on a poster displayed in the lobby. Both metrics and rewards are essential in this respect. It is essential to embed customer centric metrics, such as percent perfect order delivery, percent faultless invoices, and so on, into the firm's dashboard or scorecard, which is reviewed monthly. This also serves to diminish the second most commonly observed threat to the continuous improvement of performance through the management of the firm's large cross-functional business processes, which is the all too common trend of shifting priorities.

Accordingly, firms that excel at sustaining the gains from the improvement of large cross-functional business processes dedicate careful and thoughtful consideration to the selection of the process owner or steward for a large cross-functional process. They understand that the selected individual must be a visible and well-respected champion with the interpersonal skills needed to influence a broad range of process participants, including peers from other departments.

These firms also work to assure that process owners or stewards have the necessary support infrastructure to enable the performance monitoring and continuous improvement of the process for which they are accountable. Invariably, this involves a standing part-time process management team comprised of middle managers from the various departments involved in executing the process and a full-time process management team leader who has the focus of taking corrective action and assuring continuous improvement of that process. The members of the process management team are frequently assigned ownership of the key sub-processes.

Firms that excel at sustaining the gains from the improvement of large cross-functional business processes do so in part by aligning process performance. One way to do this is to allocate a minimum of about 30%, and up to as much as 70%, of the discretionary component of executives' and managers' bonuses to the achievement of process performance targets. This not only provides financial rewards and reinforcement, but also stimulates cross-functional collaboration.

It's equally important to put in place needed process management training, employing a common methodology. This is yet another key factor given the current trend of labor mobility and the inevitable rotation of personnel.

Air Products and Caterpillar Inc. are two of the firms that have successfully deployed process ownership. Air Products recognizes that the process owner role must address both effectiveness, whereby the right output is being delivered to customers and business owners, and efficiency, whereby costs are driven down through a focus on reducing cycle time and re-work.

George Diehl of Air Products recognizes the depth of complexity involved. He said, "It is one thing to measure and assign process owner accountabilities. But what about the interfaces with other people like business owners or the functional owners who had some of that authority and responsibility before? We have to recognize that there is a power shift going on."

That's why Air Products painstakingly defined process management as only one part, albeit an important part, of what makes the business work. Bill Cantwell, Air Products' Vice President of

Supply Chain, maintains that process owners need to:
- Articulate a process vision with key metrics
- Document the end-to-end process
- Sponsor convergence decisions
- Lead as a process zealot

Air Products is very clear on the multi-faceted nature of process ownership involving four key elements, as Table 4.5 depicts.

Leadership	Design
<ul><li>Drives strategic alignment and customer focus</li><li>Prioritizes global improvement opportunities through annual planning process</li><li>Resolves cross-process issues</li><li>Owns process education and training</li><li>Leads the change to a process-focused organization</li></ul>	<ul><li>Defines business and customer inputs & outputs of the process</li><li>Documents the process activities, and approves changes</li><li>Prioritizes enterprise process IT spending</li><li>Ensures controls are in place, validated, & tested for accurate financial reporting (SOx)</li><li>Audits work practice compliance</li></ul>
Performance	Improvement
<ul><li>Implements metrics & reports process performance</li><li>Achieves process metric targets and goals</li><li>Prioritizes performance gaps/shares successes</li><li>Provides adequate process resources</li><li>Monitors data quality</li></ul>	<ul><li>Analyzes process performance gaps</li><li>Develops plans to close gaps</li><li>Executes Continuous Improvement projects across business units</li><li>Benchmarks and adopts best practices</li><li>Fosters new continuous improvement ideas</li></ul>

Table 4.5. Air Products' Process Owner Accountability

To support the efforts of process owners, Air Products has

taken action in several critical areas. It has:

- Created a full-time position under each executive process owner called process manager,
- Institutionalized the use of a corporate scorecard with the firm's 10 key performance indicators with a line of sight to the process, functional, and strategic business unit scorecards,
- Introduced an employee training program called "Introduction to Process Management" that provides employees with the knowledge and skills needed to be active participants in the process management effort,
- Given process owners control of the IT purse strings.

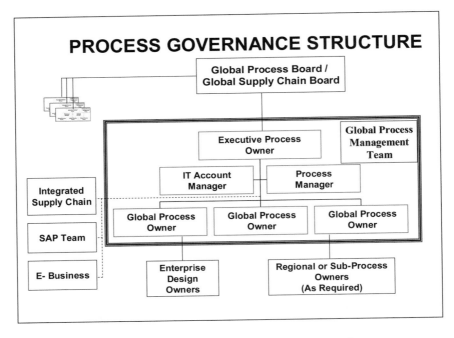

Figure 4.2. Air Products Process Governance Structure

All of these tactics are embodied in a process management governance structure that stresses interdependence and collaboration, as depicted in Figure 4.2.

Caterpillar, Inc. has also made solid progress in the institution-alization of process management. For example, in the Order Fulfillment area, it has identified governance as one of the critical success factors, as indicated on Figure 4.3.

---

1. *We must develop an Order Fulfillment structure and recipe* that pre-scribes what must be done to implement an industry-leading Order Fulfillment process.

2. *We must develop and deliver* a compelling communications message targeted at generating enthusiasm, understanding, and commitment to the successful implementation of Order Fulfillment processes at all levels of the value chain.

3. *We must understand* the customers' Order Fulfillment needs and how those needs impact the value chain.

4. *We must institutionalize* a governance model that enables trans-formation to industry-leading customer centric Order Fulfillment business processes.

5. *We must implement* a funding model for the Order Fulfillment process that prioritizes and leverages spending to optimize the value chain and delivers measurable benefits to the Enterprise.

6. *We must measure* the value chain, establish improvement targets, and maintain accountability to drive performance.

7. *We must couple* Order Fulfillment processes with industry-leading and enabling technologies to deliver solutions that maximize benefits to the value chain.

8. *We must be* a continual learning organization matching indus-try-leading Order Fulfillment knowledge with value chain needs.

Figure 4.3. Order Fulfillment Critical Success Factors at Caterpillar

Caterpillar stresses that the vision for order fulfillment at Cat-erpillar is "From order to delivery, our customers and shareholders are delighted."

Caterpillar recognizes the importance of aligning rewards.

Chuck Laurenti, Global Order Fulfillment Process Owner at Caterpillar, said in this regard, "That's one of the things we are working on hard. We have worked to align part of our compensation called the incentive – that's basically the variable part that's paid on an annual basis. But right now it's uneven. We have it aligned in some businesses and not aligned in others, because the incentive compensation is chosen and executed at an operational level in each of these 'accountable' businesses. So some have done it and others haven't. We're working towards that, because we recognize that if we don't have rewards totally aligned, we'll have a much more difficult time getting there."

What are some of the major pitfalls in deploying process management for continuous improvement? These include, but are not limited to, assigning process ownership at too low a level in the organization, failing to link customer centric, qualitative measures of performance tightly to the traditional financial measures, and underestimating the value of providing meaningful incentives to promote cross-group and/or cross-functional collaboration.

The accountability for improving the performance of key business processes is predicated on the notion of cross-functionality. The pitfall of assigning process ownership at too low a level in the organization threatens the depth of cross-functional and/or cross-group collaboration and will tend to reinforce existing functional or group silos.

A failure to link qualitative measures of performance tightly to the traditional financial measures sends the message that, at the end of the day, all that really counts is financial performance. Only by correlating the desired improvements in service quality and cycle time reduction to the traditional financial measures, and reviewing these in a disciplined manner in monthly operating reviews, can the right signal be communicated. Again, information technology has a central role to play in this regard. While sampling methods, manual estimation and correlation can work for a short period of time; eventually these tasks become burdensome in the absence of enabling technology. Fortunately, there is increasing recognition of the importance in linking business process management software to business intelligence systems.

Underestimating the value of providing meaningful incentives to promote cross-group and/or cross-functional collaboration is an easy trap to fall into. Yet, if the recognition and reward systems for the continuous improvement of a company's critical business processes are neither visible enough nor significant enough, then people will act accordingly.

Disciplined process management is what delivers operating results consistently. It provides the means for sustaining and improving the gains from process redesign projects.

Even those organizations that have made significant progress in elevating senior management attention to the enterprise business processes continue to see mindset challenges.

George Maszle, Xerox's Director, Lean Six Sigma, acknowledged that many "efforts do not achieve their full potential."[10] He indicated some of the key differentiators of success would include:

- Ability to achieve full integration into the business and "how we work;"
- Project selection linked to business strategies;
- Project selection link to customer value;
- Ability to change culture and leadership behavior;
- Engaging the full value chain in all geographies and operations;
- Ability to track results (i.e., robust Project Tracking System).

Know this: You need to understand the key phases of the methods in use within your organization and the role of the leader in each phase. Your mindset and behavior materially impact the success of improvement efforts.

Again, the overarching themes of measurement and governance are in evidence. How will you know when you are making progress? Table 4.6 illustrates.

What's Needed:
Design enterprise business processes to deliver on company goals
Signs of Progress: <ul><li>Focus on the critical few processes most in need of improvement to perform for customers</li><li>Leaders stimulate conversation on process improvement and management</li><li>Process owners chair meetings with sub-process owners and process management teams</li><li>There is increasing conversation and awareness of cross-process dependencies</li><li>People begin to assign their loyalty as much to process as to function or business</li><li>People are aware of the progress in closing the gap between current and desired performance</li><li>There is a visible decline in cross-department finger pointing</li><li>There is a visible improvement in cross-department collaboration</li></ul>

Table 4.6. Signs of Progress

To sum up this chapter, let's remember that a plan is just a plan. Converting plans into action involves the improvement and management of your company's critical business processes.

Chapter 4: Self-Assessment Questions

1. Is your process improvement project launched with a customer centric view?
2. Do you take the time and effort to compile baseline data on process performance early in the life of the project?
3. Do you set realistic schedules for the project?
4. Is there continuing dialogue between management and the project team?
5. Do you insist on having a concise, compelling vision for the new design?
6. Is the IT department engaged early in the project?
7. Is there clarity in the way in which business should be con-

ducted in the future to achieve strategic goals?
8. Do you typically develop a clear matrix of performance measures that should be monitored in the future?
9. Do you insist on having a document that details changes in roles/accountabilities and indicates this for the new process?
10. Do you typically have a high level implementation plan that indicates who will need to do what by when to install new business practices, and process changes and related technology, with approximate milestones?
11. Do you pave the way for the continuous monitoring and improvement of the process by having a strong process owner or steward and a standing process management team?
12. Are you investing in broad based training in a common process improvement methodology?

References.

[1] Harrington, James H. and K. C. Esseling and Van Nimwegen, *Business Process Improvement Workbook:: Documentation, Analysis, Design and Management of Business Process Improvement*, McGraw-Hill, 1997

[2] Davenport, Thomas H., 'Reengineering a Business Process', *Harvard Business School Publishing Case Note*, November 1995

[3] Hammer, Michael, 'The Superefficient Company', *Harvard Business Review*, September 2001

[4] Pande, Peter, S. and Robert P. Newman and Roland R. Cavanaugh, *The Six Sigma Way: How GE, Motorola and other top companies are Honing Their Performance*, McGraw-Hill, 2000

[5] This general approach reflects the method outlined in: Rummler, Geary A. and Alan Brache, *Improving Performance: How to Manage the White Space on the Organization Chart*, Jossey-Bass, 1995.

[6] Fornari, Arthur and George Maszle, 'Lean Six Sigma Leads Xerox', *Six Sigma Forum Magazine*, August 2004

[7] ibid

[8] Project Management, *The Economist*, June 11, 2005

[9] Garten, Jeffrey E., 'Jack Welch: a Role Model for Today's CEO?', *Business Week*, September 10, 2001

[10] Fornari, Arthur and George Maszle, 'Lean Six Sigma Leads Xerox', *Six Sigma Forum Magazine*, August 2004

Five

Organization Design

Every company has two organizational structures: The formal one is written on the charts; the other is the everyday relationship of the men and women in the organization.
– Harold S. Geneen

Is it necessary to reorganize in order to become a process-focused enterprise? That question is frequently asked, especially by executives steeped in tradition. As much as we may love to hate organizational hierarchies because of their inherent rigidity and the way they sometimes make us feel, some form of hierarchy or structure is not only needed, but also desirable and inevitable in today's complex organizations.

After all, the structure of a company is what determines the disposition of power and authority. It's an important element of organization design, but just one of several components, if one defines organization design as the complex relationship of structure, recognition, and rewards and not just the placement of boxes on the organization chart.

Ideally, organization design should make it easy for the customer to do business with the company, and enable employees to perform for customers. At the very least, organization design should not inhibit the ability of the company to serve the needs of customers.

That's why achieving a shared understanding of what matters to customers by measuring what counts, assigning accountability for the performance of value added work that crosses the firm's formal structural boundaries, and aligning recognition and reward systems are more important than the specific structural composition of the firm. In this paradigm, the process perspective becomes an additional, and important, dimension of management in the executive team's frame of mind, reflecting a high degree of customer focus.

While there may not be one clear-cut generic answer on the topic of organization design, some general guidelines can be established, especially if one defines organization design as the complex relationship of structure, recognition, and rewards, and not just the hierarchy on the organization chart.

Fundamental Concepts

There are several fundamental concepts that are useful to emphasize when it comes to organization design.

First, the concept of "fit" is central. The importance of "fit" among the organizational elements of strategy, structure, and processes, in order to optimize effectiveness and performance, dates back to the 1970s.[1] But it wasn't fully articulated until the mid-1990s, when it was proposed that organization design should make it easy for the customer to do business with a company, and that this design required fit among the elements of strategy, structure, processes, rewards, and people.[2] Any structure is relatively easy to copy. The fit between strategy, structure, processes, rewards, and people, as depicted in Galbraith's "Star Model," isn't.

Next, organization design should make it easy for the customer to do business with the company, and also enable employees to perform for customers. However, in so doing, there's a price to pay. Especially when it comes to large, international organizations; a design that makes it easy for customers and employees generally involves a higher level of complexity for the company's leaders.[3]

Then, contrary to the prevailing conventional wisdom, strategy should not be the only guiding force determining the preferred organization structure. Instead, in the process-oriented firm, strategy should drive process design, which in turn should dictate organization design. In this regard, process design is not just limited to the flow of information and data; but, rather, it represents the big picture view of who does what to get work done. This is a fundamental shift in thinking.

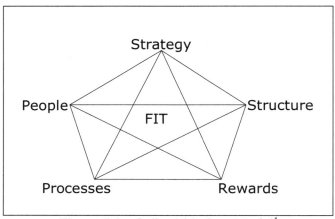

Figure 5.1. Galbraith's Star Model[4]

Fourth, any wholesale restructuring of an entire organization is deeply disruptive and should be approached with caution. Of course, this hasn't prevented many firms from frequent restructurings, with little, if any, impact on performance.

Let's also note that every form of organization structure has associated strengths and weaknesses. Those readers interested in a thorough treatment of alternative organization designs are invited to pay particular attention to Galbraith's 1995, "Designing Organizations," and the more recent publication, "Designing the Customer Centric Organization."[5]

Traditional Structural Forms

While the functional structure has come under criticism, it remains the most widespread basis of organization design in use since the industrial revolution. Its strengths include that it facilitates economies of scale within functional departments and enables in-depth knowledge and skill development in a given functional area. While it has been recognized that it is best applied within firms that offer one or a few products, it continues to be a cornerstone of organization design, even within firms who have a dominant product-driven or divisional structure. This is in spite of the widely recognized weaknesses of the functional organization design including a rigid hierarchy, which may result in slow response time to change, as well as poor horizontal coordination among departments – often considered to be one of the major obstacles to improving a company's cross-functional processes. It has been known for some time that the process of horizontal structure is a viable alternative to a functional formation.[6] Nonetheless, we have not seen the extensive adoption of the flat, networked horizontal structures, except perhaps in smaller companies. The fact that there has not been a broad based movement to replace the functional structure with a process structure in mid-sized and larger firms is a testament to the deeply entrenched nature of the traditional functional mindset, which makes it difficult to achieve a high level of collaboration across various departments.

In larger, more complex organizations, a business unit or SBU structure, based on either market segments or product groups, is more commonly observed than the traditional functional structure. The market segment structure is particularly common in service industries such as banking (corporate, commercial, retail) and telecommunications (corporate, consumer). But it is also evident in companies offering a product/service mix such as office equipment (corporate and small business) and pharmaceuticals (hospital, specialist, general). The obvious advantage of structuring according to market segment is the ability to focus more effectively on customer needs within a segment – a much needed capability given the increasing power of customers.

The product or service based structure's strengths include that it is better suited to rapid change, may lead to improved customer satisfaction because product responsibility and contact points are well defined, and it allows individual units to adapt to differences in products, regions, and customer groups. The weaknesses of the product based structure include that it involves duplication of effort and compromises potential economies of scale in functional departments, leads to poor coordination across product lines, and thereby makes integration and standardization across product lines more difficult. The most frequent criticism of the product-based structure is related to multiple sales people from different product groups calling on the same customer.

Both market segment and product based structures are often supported by a range of functional department. Also, hybrid structures are becoming increasingly common. Galbraith has written about Nokia, as an example of "front-back hybrid model."

The Finland-based firm has created a customer-centric front-end unit for SBUs such as Networks – where specific customer strategies are developed and implemented – and linked it to the product-centric units at the back end of the company.[7]

Many larger companies have adopted some form of matrix organization. The matrix structure's strengths are considered to include that it can provide more flexible sharing of human resources across products or geographies, and can represent an opportunity for both functional and product skill development. Its weaknesses are generally considered to be that it can cause people to experience frustration and confusion due to the impact of dual authority; it requires that people develop higher levels of interpersonal skills; it can be time consuming involving frequent meetings; and it generally requires significant effort and communication to maintain the balance of power and clarity on relative priorities.

The number of structural options available to large, complex companies is myriad. How much complexity can any organization absorb? The leader who wishes to examine the full range of available options would need a very large pile of paper napkins to doodle upon for what appears to be a daunting task, even without considering the best way to overlay a process or horizontal structural perspective.

The Horizontal Structure

In the absence of a clear and compelling strategy, practically any form of structure will suffice. On the other hand, given clarity on strategic direction, the decision around the precise form of structure is critical, and the process based structure or horizontal organization has a number of important advantages. Why organize by process? It facilitates:

- Focus on customer needs and the key value added outputs of the enterprise
- The alignment of process measures with management reward systems
- The reduction of the number of non-value added hand-offs for core processes
- More effective implementation of major systems projects

But there are certain things a process structure will not do. It won't eliminate the so-called "white spaces" of the organization; instead, it will simply change the number and nature of such white spaces. For example, the linkage of the product development process to the customer acquisition and engagement process and the order fulfillment process become significant. In this respect, the change of formal structure, by itself, may not dramatically alter traditional management thinking, as focused metrics and aligned rewards are needed too.

Mid-sized companies with a single or just a few product offerings are sometimes the best candidates for moving from a pure functional structure to a horizontal structure, at least for the company's primary, or customer touching, business processes. Generally, this involves a restructuring from the traditional functions of Sales, Marketing, Operations, Customer Service, and R&D to a process structure such as Customer Engagement, Order Fulfillment, and New Product Development, with the supporting functions of Finance, Human Resources, and Legal remaining as-is or being combined in a shared service organization. This can provide such firms with faster, better responsiveness to changing customer requirements, reduced cycle-time in the introduction of new products, and/or services, and better alignment in the development of enabling information systems.

But a wholesale change in the functional structure of the firm may not be needed if the firm has become adept at the use of cross-functional teams to address the ongoing improvement and management of its critical business processes, and the needed set of process measures, aligned recognition systems, and rewards are in place. In this latter case, a strong, senior level process advocate can serve to maintain focus on process performance. Perhaps that is why a number of companies such as Pitney Bowes, La-Z-Boy Incorporated, Thomson Scientific, and Electrocomponents PLC have reported having established positions such as Vice President of Process Improvement, Vice President and General Manager, Business Processes, or even Chief Process Officer.

In so doing, these companies have added somewhat of a process or horizontal dimension to what would otherwise be a traditional form of organization design. The challenge of engaging the entire executive team in taking some accountability for the company's enterprise-level processes remains nevertheless.

Viable Alternatives

For large, geographically dispersed companies, the challenge is more about accountability for performance, and alignment of the organization design elements of measures, recognition and rewards, than it is about a physical restructuring of the firm along process lines.

Air Products has taken an innovative approach, invoking the process view as a third dimension of management. With more than 20,000 employees, as of the end of 2004, it is organized around a combination of business units and functional areas.

Instead of layering a process structure on an already complex global organization, Air Products stresses what it calls the 3rd dimension of management, as depicted in Figure 5.2 below.

Process as the "third dimension of management" is a concept that's particularly useful for large, complex organizations. It has significant potential, almost irrespective of the formal structure of the multifaceted firm, be it market segment, product, hybrid, or even matrix based.

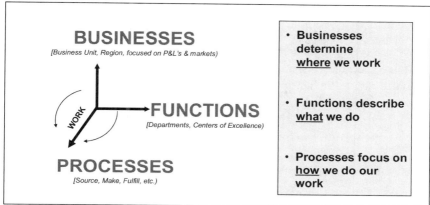

Figure 5.2. Air Products: The 3rd Dimension of Management

The 3rd dimension of management places processes in just the right context, as the means to get things done in a collaborative environment. It fully recognizes that people will naturally be loyal to the organization within which they work (the business, unit, or region) and the type of work they do (departments or centers of excellence). It does not attempt to subjugate the manager's or employee's loyalty or relationship to the business or the function. Instead, it positions the way in which work is done as a critical component of management and on the same plane as the means for achieving results for customers and shareholders.

Finding the right balance of process governance with functional responsibility is essential. For example, the Vice President of Global Customer Engagement at Air Products is also the Executive Process Owner of the Fulfill global process (order to cash process), one of the company's 13 global processes. This executive is responsible for the cross-function leadership and performance of the end-to-end process, while also leading the primary function at the heart of the process.

You will appreciate that the "third dimension of management" concept needs to be reinforced by customer-centric measures of performance, clear definition of key processes, aligned recognition and reward systems, and a common method of improving and managing "how we do our work."

In this respect, it can't just be lip service. Therefore, the degree of visibility and perceived importance of customer-centric measures of performance has to be at least on the same plane as the traditional financial measures of revenue, earnings, and cash flow.

Similarly, the definition of the key business processes has to be as clear and visible as the definition of the organization structure via the ever-present organization chart. Also, the recognition and rewards for improving how work is done for the benefit of customers must be as significant and as visible as the rewards for meeting budget. Otherwise, everyone will not know what's really important.

Some larger firms prefer to avoid physical restructuring while elevating the visibility of a process focus. Xerox – a global firm with over 58,000 employees worldwide, as of the end of 2004 – appears to recognize this complexity. It is structured along a combination of business groups and geographic operations. It has attempted to gain consistency between the functional view and the process view of the business.

As George Maszle of Xerox explained, given the inherent complexity of the enterprise, the focus is more on establishing ownership of process performance than on structural changes. He stated, "Wherever possible the ownership of business processes is consistent with the organizational or functional view of business processes. Artificial ownership is avoided wherever possible. For example, our manufacturing and supply chains have all been integrated under a worldwide organization structure. This has created clear accountability for all aspects of performance management associated with this value chain. Another example is the organizational alignment of our customer services operations under a single integrated organization structure."

Whether a company elects to deploy an approach, such as viewing process as the third dimension of management, or it simply attempts to bring into line the process view with the existing hierarchical organization, the importance of recognition and rewards system alignment can hardly be overstated.

Aligning recognition and reward systems with tangible performance for customers relies on a sustainable focus in measuring what matters to customers.

Aligning reward systems also relies on assigning a meaningful component of discretionary bonuses to the achievement of observable measurable performance improvement.

An Evolutionary Approach to Organization Design

When leaders recognize that organization design should make it easy for the customer to do business with the company, and enable employees to perform for customers, they will opt for an evolutionary approach to organization design. They will recognize that clarity on how the company can better perform for customers will yield insights on the best form of organization design for their company.

What would this involve? It requires that leaders subscribe to a set of beliefs including:

- Customer requirements should be a principle driver of strategy
- Strategy is best executed through the improvement of the organization's business processes
- Process improvement creates insights on the best form of organization design
- Organization design encompasses not only structural forms but also includes alignment of recognition and reward systems

Accordingly, an evolutionary approach requires a different set of leadership mindset and behaviors than what is the norm (see Table 5.1). There's a built-in bias to such an approach. It relies on insights from both performance measurement and process governance. Alternatives such as the use of cross-functional teams and creating greater transparency and access to data through the use of information systems become more meaningful as opposed to making structural changes. It will result in a series of incremental refinements to organization design and an evolution in aligning the various elements of organization design.

Mindset	Behavior
▪ Resist the urge to make whole-sale changes to structure prematurely ▪ Recognize the importance of "fit" among the variables of strategy, structure, processes, rewards, and people	▪ Agree on an enterprise view or schematic of the business ▪ Develop a plan on performing for customers in a process context
▪ Resist jumping to conclusions; be open to alternatives ▪ Exercise patience and use process improvement and management efforts to gain insight on structural implications	▪ Take action to improve the top priority processes ▪ Manage the set of enterprise business processes

Table 5.1. Organization Design Leadership Mindset & Behavior

Leaders who wish to evolve to a horizontal organization will become interested in finding the means to assess the degree of process orientation throughout the organization. DRK Research has developed one assessment instrument that is useful in this respect.[8] It is particularly useful as an assessment instrument for large, multi-faceted companies, but can benefit organizations of any size. This survey instrument provides the means to assess people's perceptions on a variety of critical dimensions, including the degree of adoption of a process view of the business, the dedication and visibility of process management and measurement systems, and the degree of interdepartmental conflict and interdepartmental connectedness. The instrument also attempts to assess the general perception of people on the topic of process thinking to the perceived level of organizational performance.[9]

One of the essential features of the instrument is that it provides the means to assess people's perceptions on the extent of collaboration and conflict.

Does it ever make sense to contemplate an across-the-board restructuring of the organization from a traditional form of organization to one based on process? Yes, some have argued that traditional forms of organization are no longer adequate for the current business environment.[10] However, there has not been any significant movement in this direction.

While a wholesale, massive restructuring is inherently disruptive, in certain rare instances it may make sense. It may make particular sense if the leader believes that the existing culture of the company is so deeply entrenched with traditional behaviors that it is essential to drastically "shake up" the organization. Of course, there's a price to pay. Also, such an abrupt move to a horizontal structure has to be accompanied by aligned recognition and reward systems to reinforce the focus of performing for customers.

There's No "One Size Fits All"

Whether the approach is gradual or sudden, the principal message is that there is no "one size fits all" formula when it comes to organizing around process.

So which firms are most likely to benefit from restructuring along process lines? That depends, in part, on the size, complexity, and current organization structure of the firm. In general, mid-sized companies with a single or few product offerings, serving one or two primary market segments, and currently organized on a purely functional basis, are most likely to benefit. A shift to a "horizontal" organization, supported by the needed set of measures, recognition and reward systems, and related business practices would not be deeply disruptive and would improve customer focus, compress cycle time for key activities, and thereby reduce overall costs.

Next, mid-sized and larger companies, with a single or few product offerings, serving one or two primary market segments, in a single geographic area, currently organized on a pure product basis or a product/functional hybrid structure, may wish to examine this form of structure and its potential benefits. This is mainly worth considering if the culture of the firm is so traditional that the only way to shift behavior is to disrupt the status quo dramatically. But there is a price to pay in terms of disruption.

When it comes to large, international organizations, most such firms have already injected significant complexity into the design of the company's structure. For these organizations, the concept of the "third dimension of management" may offer the means to inject process orientation without a formal restructuring. Companies already organized according to a *customer-centric* front end will find this conceptual overlay of process thinking particularly promising.

Organization design should make it easy for the customer to do business with the company, and enable employees to perform for customers. Although organization structure is important, what really counts is clear accountability for the improvement and management of the company's critical business processes, customer focused measures of performance, aligned recognition and reward systems, and broad collaboration across the formal organizational boundaries with a focus to serve the needs of customers.

How will you know when you are making progress in aligning organization design? Refer to Table 5.2.

As you consider the signs of progress in Table 5.2 below, you may observe that the essence of these signs is cultural in nature.

What's Needed: Ensure that organization design enables enterprise business process execution
Signs of Progress: • People and teams who were instrumental in improving performance for customers are recognized on a company wide basis   • The discretionary component of bonus compensation is based just as much on achieving process improvement as it is on traditional considerations   • People increasingly view the business as a series of interdependent business processes   • Process roles are increasingly emphasized in job description   • There is a visible improvement in overall "esprit de corps"

Table 5.2. Signs of Progress

The central role of culture should not come as a surprise. The design of the organization is a principal determinant of culture. Indeed, Louis Gerstner may have been right in that "culture is not just one aspect of the game – it is the game."[11]

That is why leadership mindset is so fundamental to the effective development of a robust organization design that makes it easy for the customer to do business with the company, and enables employees to perform for customers. That involves nothing less than turning the organization on its side and mobilizing the efforts of its people in customer value creation.

Chapter 5: Self-Assessment Questions

1. How often does your company restructure? Are the benefits of restructuring generally evident?
2. What dominates leadership's thinking – the customers you serve, the products you offer, or the way you are organized?
3. In general, are departments and groups collaborators or competitors?
4. Are your measurement, recognition, and reward systems designed to support the company's strategy and formal structure? Do these motivate serving the needs of customers?
5. Do you have the means to assess the degree of process orientation throughout the enterprise?

References.

[1] Galbraith, Jay R. and Daniel A. Nathanson, *Strategy Implementation: The Role of Structure and Process*, West Publishing Co., 1978
[2] Galbraith, Jay, *Designing Organizations*, Jossey-Bass, 1995
[3] Ibid
[4] Adapted from http://www.jaygalbraith.com/star_model.asp
[5] Galbraith, Jay R., *Designing the Customer-Centric Organization: A Guide to Strategy, Structure, and Process*, Wiley 2005
[6] Galbraith, Jay, *Designing Organizations*, Jossey-Bass, 1995
[7] Galbraith, Jay, 'Organizing to Delver Solutions', *Organizational Dynamic*, 5/ 2002
[8] McCormack, Kevin, Business Process Orientation, refer to http://www.drkresearch.org/Research/research.html
[9] Ibid
[10] Ostroff, Frank, *The Horizontal Organization: What the Organization of the Future Actually Looks Like and How It Delivers Value to Customers*, Oxford U. Press, 1999
[11] Gerstner, Jr., Louis V., *Who Says Elephants Can't Dance: Leading a Great Enterprise through Dramatic Change,* Harper Business, 2002

Six

The Role of Enabling Technology

The first rule of any technology used in a business is that automation applied to an efficient operation will magnify the efficiency. The second is that automation applied to an inefficient operation will magnify the inefficiency.
– Bill Gates

The role of information technology (IT) is fundamentally to enable the performance of an organization's business processes in creating value for customers and shareholders. In this day and age practically any broad based improvement effort relies extensively on IT. That's why IT is arguably the single most important enabling tool to get the most out of implementing process management, if only the traditional functional mindset didn't get in the way.

These traditional mental models and behaviors have driven executives at more than a few organizations to look for that IT silver bullet or panacea, be it an ERP or a CRM system. Instead of taking the time and energy at the outset to develop a shared understanding of which enterprise-wide business processes need to be improved, and only then determining what the role of technology should be in order to deliver on strategy, it was easier to throw problems over the wall to IT. After all, the IT folks are accountable for process and technology – right? Unfortunately, the challenges related to understanding and implementing new and complex software solutions have become so intricate that there has typically been little room in the budget or the mindset of the IT folks truly to focus on what matters from an end-to-end business process perspective.

The traditional departmental view of business has not only driven silo thinking by executives, but it has also played a role in perpetuating siloed applications thinking by IT specialists. This has led to a search for the answer to the question, "Who is ultimately accountable for technology-enabled business performance improvement at the enterprise level?" Accordingly, the question of "governance" of IT initiatives is attracting increasing attention. It was recently reported that in a survey of 276 companies, 83% of respondents indicated that their firms have either implemented or are about to implement some form of IT governance.[1]

Sustainable focus on what matters from an end-to-end business process perspective is needed. The mindset shifts needed to make this happen include:

- Performing for customers is what counts and processes are vehicles to deliver that performance.
- The central role of IT is to enable business process performance.
- End users and IT practitioners need to collaborate more effectively. They need to understand the vision of the future in the same way and work together to get it right.
- Ideally, the process should be improved before it is wrapped in expensive technology.

This is easier said than done. The business-IT relationship has been problematic for some time now. Recently, IT has come under more vocal attack.

Yet, the evolving suite of business process management software (BPM), while still immature, offers hope for the future. In the end, leadership mindset and behavior will make the difference.

The Business-IT Equation

It's sad but true that in far too many organizations, IT investments are not linked to business strategy. According to a recent survey, 77% of CFOs believe IT is strategic – but only 43% believe they will spend more on IT as a result, and only 40% of CFOs believe that the IT investments had produced the expected returns.[2]

So it comes as no surprise that IT has come under attack from many quarters since the bursting of the dot-com bubble. Arguably, the most well known attack was launched by Nicolas Carr in the May 2003 issue of *Harvard Business Review's* sensationally titled article, "IT Doesn't Matter."[3] The IT community was quick to rebut the article's contention that IT may no longer be the basis for competitive advantage. The wave of rebuttals included comments by industry luminaries such as Bill Gates of Microsoft and Intel's Craig Barrett, and even gave impulse to a book by Smith and Fingar, *IT Doesn't Matter – Business Processes Do.*[4]

Around the same time, a sprinkling of articles appeared on the need for IT to improve in terms of meeting senior executives' expectations, including an article based on research in France, "What CEOs Really Think of IT," where it was reported that "CEOs attribute the gap between expected and actual performance mainly to the insufficient involvement of business units in IT projects, to the weak oversight and management of these projects, and to IT's inadequate understanding of their business requirements."[5]

The payoff from IT initiatives is frequently perceived to be poor. There's too much technology for its own sake, and the relationship between IT users and IT practitioners is often reported to be dysfunctional. Further, due to the sheer complexity of many IT projects, one of the biggest problems is that simply getting the IT initiative done frequently replaces the originally contemplated goals. This focus on "just get it done" may be one of the reasons that the originally stated goals of major IT initiatives are often not met. The Standish Group estimated that in 2004, only 29% of IT projects were on time and on budget – down from 34% in 2002.[6]

Yet, firms depend heavily on IT to get work done. When IT fails to perform, headlines are made. This is particularly true of ERP implementations. In addition to the widely publicized case of Fox-Meyer, which attributed its bankruptcy, in part, to ERP implementation issues, two additional examples, as reported on www.cio.com, involved Hershey Foods and Whirlpool. Hershey Foods experienced massive distribution problems following a flawed implementation of their ERP system, which affected shipments to stores in the 1999 peak Halloween and pre-Christmas sales periods. In November 1999, domestic appliance manufacturer, Whirlpool of Benton Harbor, Michigan, also blamed shipping delays on difficulties associated with its ERP implementation.[7]

Advances in Technology

While concerns on ERP and CRM systems persist to this day, there have been significant advances in process-oriented technologies, including the emergence of a new category of business process management (BPM) software, frequently dubbed Business Process Management System or BPMS.

Note that BPM software is a tool set and not process management, just in the same way that CRM software was not customer relationship management.

This category of software differs from the large, monolithic ERP and CRM applications in that the focus is clearly on the automation of a given process, or, in the case of BPMS, on a set of processes. BPM software vendors claim that this generation of software has benefits that include faster, less expensive development of applications, more visibility and transparency, co-existence and enhancement of existing applications, and ease of managing change as the process evolves.

The set of IT tools available for this task are evolving rapidly and include business process management suites (BPMS) and services oriented architecture (SOA). A cornerstone of IT-enabled improvement that provides customers with "more for less" is Web-based self-service. Peter Fingar describes the essence of Web-based self-service in his book, *Extreme Competition,* as a high-touch process-powered self-service that harnesses the power of the Web to meet the needs of customers and other participants in the process, and dramatically reduce the cost of providing high quality service and support. It is predicated on an outside-in business perspective where the center of gravity is consciously shifted to the people involved in the process – such that the process responds to customers', partners' and employees' needs rather than requiring them to adapt to pre-defined, rigid processes.

Ken Vollmer, principal analyst with Forrester Research, described the evolution of the IT environment and specifically the integration of BPMS with SOA at a recent conference. The slide depicted in Figure 6.1 represents this perspective on the evolution of integration toolsets over the past 15 years.

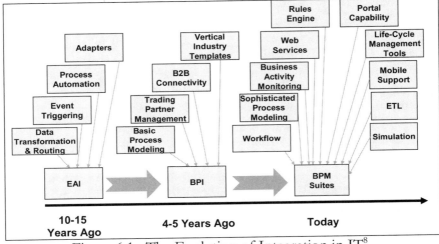

Figure 6.1. The Evolution of Integration in IT[8]

The respondents in the Mindset Study indicated that there are success stories. The CIO of a global bank said they have taken action to improve the performance compliance process around the Patriot Act and also around the Basel II Accord, where a BPM system was used to good advantage and represented "... aggressive and interesting use of BPM technology where instead of taking years to do it, we used BPM to rapidly normalize the data and we rapidly created what is essentially a large global database for all customer relations. Without BPM we couldn't have done it otherwise."

The vice president of technology of a petroleum company provided another example of a favorable experience with process improvement and the use of enabling technology. He said,

One of our real goals was to get people to do their jobs without worrying about our ERP system or the underlying systems and get people to focus on their tasks. So with this BPM product, we modified their work portal to kind of look the way our intranet looks, so people didn't have any idea what the underlying piping is or what it is doing, they just did their job and that's really been our focus from the end-user experience. Not worrying about the ERP, whether you like the ERP or you don't like the ERP, here's the work, here's the things you've got to do and we wanted to build a front-end portal to keep people from logging on to this system and logging on to that system, etc.

That's why analyst groups such as Forrester Research are paying increasing attention to this segment to the point of assessing the capabilities of various vendors in studies such as the 2004 report, "How Do the BPM Pure Plays Stack Up?"[9]

While the BPM system market has garnered significant attention, the BPM system tools' market size is currently estimated around $1.3 to $1.5 billion. This is only a drop in the bucket when one examines the billions spent on IT. Forrester Research estimates that spending on software in the US alone is around $116 billion in 2005.[10]

There is little doubt that the technology is evolving. But there is ample room for progress when it comes to executive engagement in the implementation of enabling technology. Note that it's not about support; it's about *active engagement*.

There's plenty of executive support for IT and technology generally. Company executives approve millions of dollars to be spent on it. In fact, sometimes it seems like there is still too much support for the IT panacea. What too few businesses and IT executives do is to start with a solid understanding of what business processes need to be improved by how much to create value for customers. BPM software vendors often report that executive vision, full engagement, solid project management, and user involvement remain critical success factors for project success, just as in traditional IT deployments. The views of two BPM technology firms reflect a high degree of alignment in this respect as Table 6.1 depicts.

The Fuego Perspective	The Metastorm Perspective
What are the top business practices that successful companies do in implementing BPM?	**What are the top business practices that successful companies do in implementing BPM?**
■ **Executive Sponsorship is Key** - It is important to enlist the active cooperation and participation of many individuals in the organization. Therefore you must secure the appropriate level of sponsorship.	■ **Have Executive Vision and Support** – The organizations that are most successful in implementing BPM and seeing real ROI from BPM are those that have executive buy-in from the onset of the project and have a vision for improving processes across the organization.
■ **Correctly Scope the Project** - Begin by focusing on a key business area within the organization, with a clearly defined problem, objective, and timeframe. Later you can expand the scope.	■ **Establish a Close-Knit Business & IT Team** – Business Process Management initiatives are largely driven by business users who have a need to improve a particular process; however, IT support is
■ **Start with the End in Mind** - Be aware of the business problem, the scope, and the goal that the sponsor defined at the start of the discovery project. This will prevent you from acquiring facts that may be irrelevant to the problem at hand.	absolutely critical to ensuring that BPM technology is implemented correctly and is integrated to all of the necessary systems to fully automate a cross-functional process and ensure end-to-end process visibility. Any attempt to implement BPM without both Business and IT leadership and support will likely fail.
■ **Framework** - Choose a framework that is appropriate for the organization and for your problem. Whatever framework you choose must be thoroughly understood, agreed to, and clearly communicated to your sponsor and to all participants in the process activities.	■ **Focus on High-Value Processes** – To get the best results from BPM, organizations must apply the technology to high-value, mission critical processes. This is the best way to deliver tangible financial results and to demonstrate the value of BPM to other parts of the organization in order to expand the implementation into an enterprise-wide initiative.
■ **Engage Stakeholders** - During the interviews and analysis, make sure you have interviewed the key owners and participants in the processes. Be sure to communicate with upstream and downstream process owners as well. Ensure that the IT Group participates as required to capture data and system attributes. Review end-to-end processes and key analytical results with the relevant stakeholders for their review, buy-in and validation.	

Table 6.1. Success factors in deploying BPM technology

While an enterprise view is likely to yield the most significant benefits of deploying information technology, some companies have been able to harvest impressive gains by deploying BPM software on a project-by-project basis.

This is illustrated by the case of Tenet Healthcare. Tenet began to explore the application of BPM in 2003. At that time, many of its IT systems were characterized by multiple platforms, limited functionality, lack of flexibility, and they were difficult to maintain. Tenet was attracted to deploying BPM applications as a single solution as it offered the prospect of faster time to market, more robust functionality, greater flexibility, and ease of maintenance. It implemented several projects over the period 2003 through 2005 and realized some significant benefits. Todd Coffee, Director of Business Process Management, said, "At Tenet, our projects are demand driven. We focus on providing increased throughput, reduced cycle time, and increased compliance. The use of BPM has resulted in development cycle times being greatly reduced while improving the quality and functionality of our applications. The result has been a doubling of demand from the business side." For example, on one project, the submission-to-check process was reduced from multiple weeks to as little as one day. In another case, it was able to reduce the request-to-access process from several days to as low as a few hours. If such gains are possible from implementing individual projects, then the prospects for a broader perspective are potentially exciting.

What's Needed?

From a senior management perspective, the good news is that there is very little wrong with IT that a healthy dose of *business process thinking* by senior line executives and IT practitioners wouldn't go a long way toward fixing.

If you agree that it's time that executive leadership share accountability for the deployment of IT, then there are four aspects to a new and more effective way of thinking and acting:

- Articulate the firm's strategy in terms of the performance of its end-to-end, enterprise business processes.
- Define the observable and quantifiable improvement to busi-

ness process performance and assess the deployment of enabling technology accordingly and maintain focus on these
through to successful implementation.

- Create a certain degree of shared accountability by business unit
  and technical executives for the deployment for information
  technology.
- Modify the management reward systems so that some part of
  executive compensation is based on enterprise business process
  performance.

While each of these is essential, articulating the firm's strategy
in terms of the performance of its enterprise business processes is
arguably the absolute prerequisite. Of course, this requires that the
leadership team make the time and energy to define the firm's
cross-functional, end-to-end business processes at the enterprise
level and define current measures of performance for each – both
from the customer's and the company's perspectives. This exercise
allows leaders to explore answers to vital business questions: What
output does a given business process provide to customers? What
do customers expect? How are we doing relative to customer expectations? What are the major steps and handoffs in these large
cross-departmental enterprise business processes? What are the interdependencies with other business processes? What implications
are there for technology, training, and communication? Only when
answers to these tough questions are postulated is it possible to set
the stage for a tight integration of IT investments to strategy.

The deployment of enabling technology must then be defined
and assessed in terms of the observable and quantifiable improvements to business process performance. Again, this requires a
shared understanding of which business processes need to perform
at what levels in order to deliver on business goals. Enabling technology decisions require asking and answering a series of key business questions: Which projects are likely to have the greatest impact
on achieving current strategy? What is the best sequence for deploying enabling technology? Are we clear on how IT initiatives will be
measured in terms of the value added to business process perform-

ance with metrics around improvements in time, cost, quality, and productivity? Is technology selected based on a pre-defined improvement objective and the extent to which it will support the people doing the work? How many concurrent projects can the organization reasonably sustain? Which projects are worthy – but simply cannot be done at this time?

Although commonsensical and straightforward, this level of process awareness is significantly different from organizations managed according to traditional, functional lines.

In traditionally managed companies, the responsibility for developing an IT strategy is often delegated to the senior IT executive and the IT staff. Because IT specialists are often more knowledgeable about technology than they are about the business, a lack of clarity on the business benefits of IT initiatives and the proliferation of IT projects are common results. This is aggravated, of course, by the fact that the business people don't fully understand fundamental IT issues. As one CIO explained, some of his peers say, "I don't know what you're talking about half the time – just fix this, will you? Just make it better."

So, it's no surprise that there's some finger pointing at the IT department in traditional organizations when projects don't deliver on time or meet expectations. One way to create collaboration and assure that IT enables process performance is to place control of the budget dollars for critical information technology deployments in the hands of the people accountable for process performance. That's precisely what has happened at Air Products, where the company has taken all IT spending from the businesses and given it to the process owners. At Air Products, the process owners are responsible for process convergence activities such that, for example, the process owner for "fulfill" (order to cash) ensures that all orders are processed in a similar way.

Business process thinking increases the chances that the leadership team will take its rightful accountability for IT investments as the top team develops a shared understanding of the performance gaps in the execution of key enterprise-wide business processes. By creating a certain degree of shared accountability with both business unit and technical executives for the deployment for IT, senior management can acquire a clearer sense of whether and where technology will enable true performance improvements. With this knowledge, they can make more informed decisions on which IT projects should be funded, what results can be expected, and what the likely pay-back might be. This approach shifts thinking from individual applications and departments to customer focus and business process performance.

Possibly the toughest hurdle to implementing business process thinking at the top is the need to modify senior management rewards. In many organizations there seems to be a real reluctance to base some portion of senior management compensation on business process performance. On the other hand, this linkage is critical to reinforce the commitment to business process thinking and behavior. Remember the old adage, "What gets measured gets done – what gets rewarded gets done consistently."

There may be light at the end of the tunnel. The increasing sophistication and ease of use of modeling tools, along with the Sarbanes-Oxley driven visibility of process, is driving more interest in a more comprehensive process perspective.

The use of process modeling as an approach to achieve the required visibility for processes both at the enterprise level and as part of business process improvement projects appears to be increasing. While flowcharting and process mapping as a means to visualize a business process have been around for some time, the current generation of "process *modeling*" tool sets claim to offer a more disciplined, standardized, consistent, and overall more scientific approach. Process modeling tools have a level of scalability and can be configured such that a bridge between IT capabilities and business requirements can be represented graphically.

Dr. Michael Rosemann of The Queensland University of Technology summarizes as many as 22 typical pitfalls observed in larger process modeling projects, and proposes certain corrective actions. Dr. Rosemann's message is clear. Modeling has a role to play if it's done rapidly and collaboratively to drive a deeper understanding of the way in which work gets done — and not just done for its own sake. The pitfalls examined by Rosemann are related to a broad range of topics on the impact of process modeling, including, strategy and governance, stakeholders, tools and related requirements, the practice of modeling, the design of to-be models, and other modeling and maintenance issues. It's important to note that Rosemann's pitfall relate to "process modeling" and not process management. The process modeling pitfalls related to strategy, governance, and stakeholders are outlined in Table 6.2.

Common Modeling Pitfalls	What to Do
▪ Lack of Strategic Connections	▪ Establish and maintain a clear and widely shared understanding of the contribution being made by process modeling to the better execution of corporate strategy.
▪ Lack of Governance	▪ Governance, i.e., accountability and decision processes related to process modeling, requires a clear specification and has to be adapted with changes in the objectives, scope or size of the modeling initiative.
▪ Lack of Synergies	▪ Be aware of all stakeholders with potential interest in modeling, and try to migrate them to one platform.
▪ Lack of Qualified Modellers	▪ Business process modeling requires specific skills, which are different from the classical profile of a business analyst.
▪ Lack of Qualified Business Representatives	▪ The right mix of business representatives is crucial for the project success.
▪ Lack of User Buy-in	▪ Make sure that the way you visualize your models is well accepted by your users.

Table 6.2. Modeling Pitfalls[11]

The Sarbanes-Oxley Act also has the potential to contribute to the needed change in thinking in the executive suite, for the pain of externally imposed accountability is indeed a great motivator. It is certainly raising the profile of process, but it is less clear whether it is leading to genuine process thinking and process-based management. Many companies have elected to use databases, including Access and Excel, to provide the basis of their SOx related documentation. Material processes have been "listed" rather than documented, an approach that is going to be difficult and costly to maintain and sustain. It is just compliance for compliance's sake.

As companies gravitate to the use of process modeling tools as the basis of their SOx documentation, they may uncover some of the following benefits:

- The ability to model material processes with their associated risks and controls
- Greater clarity on the need for process, and control owners
- Clear line of light into control gaps
- Senior executive attention being more focused on process
- A foundation of process models that can be used for both process improvement and management

However, this will only occur if firms go beyond simple compliance and adopt a "performance improvement" mindset, and this requires a closer working relationship between the CIO, the CFO, and the rest of the top management team. Are the demands of Sarbanes-Oxley promoting a closer working relationship between finance and IT? Not quite yet. A recent survey in CFO Magazine indicates that only 34% of CFOs believe that Sarbanes-Oxley is fostering a closer working relationship between finance and IT.[12]

For Sarbanes-Oxley to have an impact, it is not enough for it to lead to process documentation. It must also drive increasing interest and skill in process improvement and, ultimately, in process management.

How difficult is it to make these transitions and instill business process thinking? To be candid, it involves a lot of hard work and will make some traditional executives extremely uncomfortable.

However, the benefits far outweigh the discomfort and can improve the organization's chances of realizing a significantly better ROI on IT investments.

Business process thinking at the enterprise level makes it possible for the executive team to gain greater clarity on strategic direction, create a more robust measurement framework, gain insights into organization alignment, and get more out of enabling technology. [13] In this manner, business process thinking serves to assure that IT investments are more closely linked to the company's business strategy, and that the payoff from IT investments is directly derived from the specific improvements in business process performance. It will also minimize the chances that technology is implemented for its own sake, and improve the relationship between IT users and IT practitioners – ensuring that IT matters in your organization. How will you know when you're making progress? See Table 6.3.

What's Needed: Deploy information technology based on the value added to enterprise business process performance
Signs of Progress: • People feel there is a stronger alignment between business priorities and the IT project list • People begin to talk as much about improving performance for customers through IT enablers as they do about applications • IT people talk increasingly in business terms about performing for customers • The IT-business divide is no longer a topic of conversation • Greater data visibility and transparency due to enabling IT systems are celebrated

Table 6.3. Signs of Progress

The themes of focus and collaboration were emphasized in the article, "Getting IT Right." The authors stressed that there are three independent, interrelated, and universally applicable principles for executing IT effectively – a long term IT renewal plan linked to corporate strategy, a simplified, unifying technology platform employing the use of a clean, horizontally oriented architecture designed to serve the needs of the company as a whole, and a highly performance oriented IT organizations. Equally significant, it is the role of top management to understand and work collaboratively to apply these principles.[14]

The role of the CIO will need to evolve in order for a company to successfully deploy information technology based on the value added to enterprise business process performance. As Peter C. McCormick, Chief Information Officer at the Sumitomo Mitsui Banking Corporation, said, "This has to involve more focus on the tangible business results." That way, "you get more play than focusing [just] on the technology."

Chapter 6: Self-Assessment Questions

1) Does your CIO actively participate with the executive team in formulating strategy?

2) Has strategy been expressed and broadly communicated in business process terms?

3) Are decisions around IT investments made based on the expected and clearly documented improvement to operating performance?

4) Does your leadership team take some reasonable degree of shared accountability for the success of IT initiatives?

5) Are IT initiatives judged and expressly measured in terms of the added value to business process performance with metrics around improvements in time, cost, quality, productivity?

6) Have business processes been analyzed for improvement opportunities based on non-IT as well as IT solutions?

7) Is technology selected based on a pre-defined improvement objective and the extent to which it will support the people doing the work?

8) Are measurement methods for process improvement designed before the IT-enabled process improvements are made?

9) Are your IT systems designed such that they make best use of knowledge that people doing the work already possess?

10) Are your IT projects generally staffed with cross-functional representation?

11) Is IT project progress reported and discussed in your monthly operating reviews?

References.

[1] Violino, Bob, 'Power Steering', *CFO-IT Magazine*, Spring 2005

[2] Leibs, Scott, 'Still Waiting', *CFO Magazine*, December 2005

[3] Carr, Nicholas G., 'IT Doesn't Matter', *Harvard Business Review*, May 2003, pg 41-49.

[4] Smith, Howard and Peter Fingar, *IT Doesn't Matter – Business Processes Do*, Meghan-Kiffer Press, September, 2003, www.bpm3.com/hbr

[5] Monnoyer, Eric, "What CEO's Really Think of IT," *The McKinsey Quarterly*, 2003 Number 3

[6] *The Economist*, June 11, 2005, page 57

[7] 'ERP Training Stinks', *CIO Magazine*, June 1, 2000, see http://www.cio.com/archive/060100_erp.html

[8] BPM & SOA: A Look Into the Future, Forrester Research

[9] Leaver, Sharon, 'How do the BPM Pure Plays Stack Up', Forrester Research, March 19, 2004

[10] Bartels, Andrew, 'Expect a Tech Slowdown Before the Next Boom', Forrester Research, October 11, 2005

[11] Rosemann, Michael, 'Pitfalls of Process Modeling', to be published in the first issue of the *Business Process Management Journal* in 2006.

[12] Leibs, Scott, 'Still Waiting', *CFO Magazine*, December 2005

[13] Spanyi, Andrew, 'Business Process Management is a Team Sport', Anclote Press, 2003

[14] Feld, Charlie S., and Donna B. Stoddard, 'Getting IT Right', *Harvard Business Review*, February 2004.

Seven

Measurement

Any measurement must take into account the position of the observer. There is no such thing as measurement absolute, there is only measurement relative.
– Jeanette Winterson

A company has little hope of providing customers with "more for less" if it doesn't even measure on a sustainable basis how it is currently doing in performing for its customers. This requires the tight linkage of qualitative, customer centric metrics to traditional financial measures in monthly operating reviews.

The development of leadership mindset and behavior with respect to constantly measuring what matters most to customers is arguably the single most important enabler in providing customers with "more for less."

It is generally acknowledged that the disciplined practice of measuring the right set of performance metrics is fundamental to the formulation and implementation of strategy, as it provides the needed focus for improvement initiatives and lays the foundation for the alignment of recognition and reward systems. While an increasing number of companies consider measuring performance from a customer's perspectives in preparing for strategy formulation, far fewer continue this measurement practice throughout the year.

Similarly, it is common practice to measure performance from a customer's perspective in preparing for a process improvement project, and far less common to maintain this measurement practice as part of ongoing business operations.

Transformation of the traditional mindset is once again instrumental. The traditional mindset promotes at least two types of counterproductive leadership behaviors when it comes to measurement. The first of these is measurement myopia. People with myopia, or nearsightedness, are unable to see distant objects clearly. They have to squint. Organizations with measurement myopia are unable to view clearly what matters most to customers. That's because these organizations continue to focus myopically mostly on the traditional measures of performance – revenues, profit, cash flow, and departmental actual to budget comparisons.

While measurement of these traditional financial metrics is important, those organizations that focus *exclusively* on such traditional financial metrics risk not only the dangers of nearsightedness but also those of hind-sightedness and loss of peripheral vision. That means that these companies run a serious risk of being blindsided.

The second type of counterproductive leadership behavior when it comes to measurement can be compared to "blurred vision." When people have blurred vision it is related to the lack of sharpness of vision and can also be an important clue to eye disease. When organizations attempt to measure far too many performance metrics it can lead to the company experiencing blurred vision, and this stands in the way of clarity and focus.

In theory, there is good news, however, and a possible cure for both of these ailments, and it all revolves around the concepts of balance and relevance.

On the Concept of Balance

Over the past decade the use of the management tool, the Balanced Scorecard (BSC), has become widespread. The originators of the BSC wrote, "The name reflected the balance between short and long-term financial and non-financial measures, between lagging and leading indicators, and between external and internal performance perspectives."[1]

The following passage from the opening chapter of Kaplan and Norton's book, *The Balanced Scorecard,* presents one of the more amusing and vivid examples of the need for balance in performance measurement.

Imagine entering the cockpit of a modern jet airplane and seeing only a single instrument there. How would you feel about boarding the plane after the following conversation with the pilot?

Q: I'm surprised to see you operating the plane with only a single instrument. What does it measure?

A: Airspeed. I'm really working on airspeed this flight.

Q: That's good. Airspeed certainly seems important. But what about altitude? Wouldn't an altimeter be helpful?

A: I worked on altitude for the last few flights and I've gotten pretty good on it. Now I have to concentrate on proper air speed.

Q: But I notice you don't even have a fuel gauge. Wouldn't that be useful?

A: You're right, fuel is significant, but I can't concentrate on doing too many things well at the same time. So on this flight I'm focusing on air speed. Once I get to be excellent at air speed, as well as altitude I intend to concentrate on fuel consumption on the next set of flights.[2]

The message is clear. Navigating a corporation in today's complex business environment is at least as intricate as flying a jet airplane, and a full set of instruments is required. What's needed in measuring business performance is a broader view of business and greater balance in performance measurement.

It has been reported that more than 50% of Fortune 1000 firms have used the BSC in some form and that it has a higher adoption rate than many other well-known management tools.[3]

According to BSC proponents, the benefits of adopting the BSC include:

- Greater awareness of the team effort needed among organizational functions to implement the firm's strategy
- Better understanding of the linkages between specific organizational decisions and actions, and the chosen strategic goals
- More clarity around the firm's relationships with customers
- Better preparedness to reengineering business processes

On the other hand, it has been reported that there are critics of the BSC who have commented, "It became just a number-crunching exercise by accountants after the first year;" "It is just the latest management fad and is already dropping lower on management's list of priorities as all fads eventually do;" "We found it very complex to implement;" and "If scorecards are supposed to be a measurement tool, why is it so hard to measure their results?"[4]

In theory, there is a lot to be said for the concept of balance intrinsic to the BSC, and the originators' recent writing around the use of BSC and "strategy maps" places the notion of process thinking as central to success. In practice, the deployment of management tools such as the BSC faces implementation challenges similar to the implementation of any management tool set.

Angel and Rampersad outlined the following ten reasons for challenges in implementing balanced scorecards:

- "Emphasis on financial measures rather than non-financial, leading to measures that do not connect to the drivers of the business and are not relevant to performance improvement

- Too many objectives defined and too many performance metrics being measured to enable the organization to prioritize improvement steps adequately

- Poor data on actual performance, negating most of the effort invested in defining performance measures by not being able to monitor actual changes in results from changes in behavior

- Inadequate linkage between the critical success factors of the organization and the personal critical success factors of individual employees — creating human capital tensions between work and non-work aspirations

- Managers not communicating the cultural change clearly and continuously, supported by management deeds that confirm that management is serious

- An employee mentality that is hostile to management messages (the obverse of the previous point), often because communications have tended to be one-way and forced on an unwilling labor force

- An employee compensation plan that focuses too much on the money side and not enough on delivering organizational values, leading to a 'what's in it for me' culture

- A business strategy that is poorly understood and therefore impossible to execute — it may also be either inflexible, not keeping pace with changes in the marketplace or too flexible, causing

confusion because of frequent changes in direction and an un-
manageable scope

- An implementation plan that is not grounded in reality and unable to respond quickly to unforeseen events
- A climate of defensiveness and mistrust that leads project participants to respond to missed deadlines and overspent budgets
with buck-passing, bitterness and scapegoat-finding"[5]

Whether you subscribe to the BSC or not, Kaplan and Norton's work has done much to increase awareness for the need for
companies to balance the focus on the traditional financial metrics
of performance with non-financial measures of what's important to
customers.

But it's about more than just balance as the above list implies.
Relevance, prominently displaying actual performance results versus
targets, cascading scorecards to the process, department, and even
the team level are equally essential.

Beyond Balance

How to achieve the requisite levels of balance and relevance
without undue complexity is the challenge. The process view provides part of the answer in representing a two dimensional view of
performance. In the process view, what really counts is performing
for customers and for the company. That involves measuring the
factors that are meaningful to customers, such as perfect delivery,
responsiveness, etc., and the traditional financial metrics that are
meaningful to the company.

In addition to reinforcing customer focus, the process view
also provides organizations a better way to connect their activities
to financial results. The ability to translate customer-facing activities
into tangible financial terms is something that has eluded many who
have used the balanced scorecard in a traditional way.[6]

You have probably observed that some subject matter experts
advocate a simpler, more direct approach to measurement. Stephen
G. Smith, Senior Vice President and Managing Executive for the
Rummler-Brache Group, emphasizes the value of a simple and re-

peatable approach to measuring process performance. Smith acknowledges the importance of some of the conceptual aspects of balanced scorecard (BSC), such as aligning meaningful metrics to corporate strategy and using a balance of leading and lagging indicators. But he also stresses the importance of a metrics system with a focus on the critical few measures of performance. He emphasizes the importance of rapidly setting metrics targets and then revising such targets regularly (since you probably won't get it right the first time). Smith also underlines the crucial importance of having clearly established roles, responsibilities, and accountability in the metrics system.

What Smith and others highlight is that the outputs of a company's key business processes create context for both customer and internal business process measures of performance.

Just consider this example. Every company wants to measure its performance in delivering products or services to customers because perfect order delivery is central to customer satisfaction and repeat orders. The process in question is the order to delivery process, sometimes called order fulfillment. It begins with the receipt of an order and ends with the product or service delivered to a customer. The end of process output is "product/service delivered." From the customer's perspective, what's important is that the order be delivered when it was requested, and that the order be complete, accurate, and defect free. From the company's perspective, it is important to measure what's important to customers, but it is also important to measure what's important to the company. This may include the cost per order, the profit per order, the level of productivity (i.e., the number of orders processed per hour or per day) and possibly the firm's safety performance as measured by the number of days of lost time due to on the job accidents incurred in picking, packing, and shipping orders.

This simple example illustrates that the end of process output, in this case for the "order to delivery" process, provides the context for both the metrics that matter to the customer and those that matter to the company.

But there's an additional important point to note. The process context also enables the cascading of the key metrics to a more granular level to provide the context for diagnosis. For a typical B2B manufacturing firm, the "order to delivery" process is typically comprised of several sub-processes, including order taking, order making, order picking and packing, and order shipping. The process perspective allows a firm to identify the elements of accuracy, cost, timeliness, and productivity for each of these sub-processes as they combine to produce the final end of process output, which creates value for both the customer and the company.

Now it's true that if you were to survey dozens of companies on their enterprise level strategic measures, you would be likely to find that many looked very similar on the surface. These would invariably include metrics that represented a perspective on items such as market share, revenue, earnings, cash flow, customer satisfaction, and cost reduction. These high-level enterprise measures of performance take shape only when there is an appreciation of the size of the gap between current and desired performance and the degree of interdependence among the business processes that create value. It is the enterprise process view, discussed above in Chapter 3, that provides the means to achieve the needed level of clarity and balance.

The key principles that are essential in applying process thinking for greater balance and relevance include an integrated view, focus on the critical few measures, and prominent visibility.

For example, Air Products has superimposed selected key metrics on the supply chain component of its enterprise process blueprint as depicted in Figure 7.1 below.

An integrated, common view is critical. It sounds easy in theory, yet is problematic in practice. It is common to see companies deploying multiple management tools and initiatives at the same time. A case in point is the example of a large Canadian insurance company. This company had concurrent initiatives on "voice of the customer," "balanced scorecard," and "process improvement." You might think that the key metrics from the "voice of the customer" initiative would be fully represented in the customer quadrant of the balanced scorecard, and the key metrics from the process improvement initiatives be fully represented in the internal business process quadrant of the balanced scorecard. But they weren't. In fact, the three separate teams working these three initiatives rarely had contact with one another. If the company had an integrated view of performance, this would not have been the case.

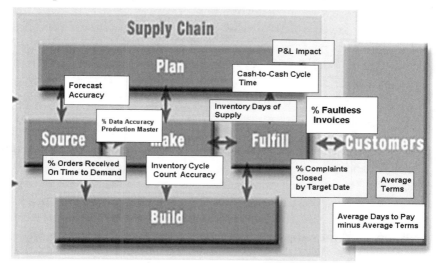

Figure 7.1. Air Products' Supply Chain Key Metrics

A focus on the critical few measures of performance is another key factor. Although this sounds easy on the surface, it represents a major challenge for many organizations because it involves making tough choices. The challenge of what truly counts to customers is even more complex in certain industries such as health care, as Jim Conway, the former Chief Operating Officer of the Dana Farber Cancer Institute, explains:

We use dashboards – but it is not institutionalized yet. We are beginning to believe – In God we trust – all others must show data. But there's a lot more work to do. We have been good on process measures (lead time, defect related quality measures) – but less so on outcome measures – i.e., effectiveness… We did the largest study that has ever been done on patient ambulatory care. We found out that we had one of the lowest error rates – but if we looked at harm and reframed it – then we found that 30 percent of our patients had significant harm from their chemotherapy – so let's stop focusing on errors and start focusing on toxicity and harm.

Difficult choices need to be made when it comes to measurement and performance improvement, even when a firm has clarity around the key business processes that create value for customers and shareholders. It is common to hear that there should not be more than 20 or so high level performance measures that the top team needs to monitor as part of its operating reviews. The challenge of monitoring twenty or more key measures at the top team level is significant.

Monitoring seven to ten top-level metrics is much more realistic. Also, the practice of using dashboards with green, yellow, and red light indicators, which has gained broad acceptance, facilitates focus and discussion only on those aspects of the business where corrective action is required. This also serves to enhance visibility.

Relevance can best be achieved when the principal performance metrics are employed as the foundation for recognition and reward systems. When companies fail to recognize and reward the teams of people who improve performance for customers, they send a clear message to employees that what counts most is the financial performance of the firm. They should then not be surprised if employees act accordingly.

Prominently displaying the company's progress on key metrics is another critical success factor. Ed Maggio of RSA Security explains how this firm uses measures to maintain focus and visibility with respect to the firm's order fulfillment process.

> For us, the highest-level measure is the delivery to commit, that is, on-time delivery performance. But we've got a number of quality measurements, we've got at one level a set of charts we do on a weekly basis, then we have a number of quality council meetings we do on a monthly basis. Everything is done in a dashboard fashion on a weekly basis, and we run everything from the on-time delivery, as we previously mentioned, to what's called same day order entry, revenue achievement, build plan achievement, bookings level achievement, and then we got more in the process quality topic, various yields, returned goods, what percent of

orders are returned.

We assure visibility in two different ways; these are posted out in the main hallway, the lobby area. Then on a quarterly basis we do a quality scorecard, which covers some selected topics, as I just mentioned. Now in the customer support area, we do a customer satisfaction rating, as well as how long is the cycle time to close cases. These, plus around 8 other key metrics, are put together in a scorecard that's presented to our executive staff. That's done on a quarterly basis.

The visibility I think allows people to focus in on it, either to be proud or take corrective action quickly. It reduces the cycle time for corrective action.

In addition to failing to focus on the critical few measures of performance, what are some of the other common pitfalls in developing an effective measurement framework? These include, but are not limited to, using measures that are vague or subject to interpretation, failing to link the measures across the value chain, failing to automate the measurement system, and failing to link the top tier of metrics tightly to operating reviews.

Viewing the business from the perspective of the enterprise business processes that create value for customers can provide the *corrective lenses* for both organizational measurement myopia and blurred vision. Why? Simply because adopting process management principles requires that a company view and measure the business' performance from the customer's point of view – looking at things outside-in, as well as from the traditional, internal perspective.

This requires focus on key principles such as an integrated view, focus on the critical few measures, prominent visibility, and relevance. It requires that the enterprise performance measurement system be tightly linked to budgets and operating reviews, as Table 7.1 depicts.

What's Needed: An integrated view, focus on the critical few measures, balance, visibility, and relevance.
What's Involved: • Include customer centric metrics in monthly operating reviews • Establish a keen focus on the top 4-7 enterprise level metrics • Develop the means to cascade metrics to the next level for rapid diagnosis • Use the principal performance metrics as the foundation for recognition and reward systems • Express the impact of improving process performance in financial terms

Table 7.1. Measurement

The role of information technology is central to the tight linkage of qualitative, customer centric metrics to traditional financial measures in monthly operating reviews. In this respect, the new generation of BPM software products also needs the capability to support decision-intensive business processes like order fulfillment or order management, and new product development. As a recent Forrester Research article recommended, it's essential to understand that:

- Sustainable performance management cannot exist without business process capabilities
- Business process monitoring, reporting, and optimization requires decision-intensive analytics[7]

As organizations become more adept in establishing a sustainable focus on measuring what matters most to customers and to the organization, they will also begin to explore dependencies and ask more meaningful "what if" questions.

Only the most advanced firms have even thought about questions such as, "If we improve perfect order delivery by 3%, what will the impact be on our 'days of sales outstanding' or DSO and our 'cash to cash cycle time'?" Or, "If we could compress new product enhancement cycle time by 25%, what would the impact then be on revenues and profits from new products?" Yet, it is precisely such questions that strike to the interdependent nature of complex business processes that will take companies to the next level of sophistication in measurement. And it is the process view that provides the needed context.

For most organizations it's not a short journey. When asked, "To what extent is there a shared understanding of process performance by the leadership team?" Øystein Risan, director of Operations at NSB said, "Not significantly. I think we are beginning to get there in Operations. Most of the leaders still think in terms of organizational structures as opposed to processes."

Measurement, when deployed on a sustainable basis, is not only a prerequisite for providing customers with "more for less," it is also the key to discipline for an organization to achieve focus and alignment. The role of measurement in achieving focus, while critical, is self-evident. Its role in aligning the efforts of the entire organization through recognition and reward systems may be more subtle, but no less important.

Sustainable emphasis on measuring the output of the activities that create value for customers can accelerate this essential transition. How will you know when you're making progress? See Table 7.2.

What's Needed: Tightly link the enterprise performance measurement system to budgets and operating reviews

Signs of Progress:
- There's just as much discussion on the progress in improving performance for customers in operating reviews as on the traditional financial measures
- People talk increasingly about improvements to perfect order delivery and responsiveness
- Current performance on critical to customer metrics are prominently displayed
- Leaders ask "what if" questions around the impact of process performance on financial metrics

---

Table 7.2. Signs of Progress

The themes of measurement and governance recur with regularity in any thorough treatment of process management. Measuring what matters to customers and assuring accountability in performing for customers is one of the major challenges that must be addressed. However, changing traditional practice takes patience and persistence. That's why many firms find that making progress in these areas is more like a journey, not a sprint.

Chapter 7: Self-Assessment Questions

1. Has your leadership team identified the critical few measures of performance that need to be monitored?
2. Is there good balance between a focus on the traditional financial metrics of performance and the non-financial measures of what's important to customers?
3. Is there a shared understanding among the top team members on the relative priority of these performance metrics?
4. Is there adequate discipline exercised in the monthly review of the company's key performance metrics?
5. Is there good visibility of the progress towards strategic objectives?
6. Are the key performance metrics used to align recognition and reward systems?
7. Have key performance measures been cascaded to sub-process, team, division, and functional levels?
8. Do you typically use reference sources such as the APQC PCF and the SCC SCOR to stimulate thinking about the definition and measurement of macro process blocks?
9. Do you typically use reference sources such as the set of metrics in the Supply Chain Council's SCOR to stimulate thinking about the best baseline metrics to employ in process improvement projects?
10. Do you typically use available reference sources to stimulate thinking about the full range of metrics to be used in measuring the performance of major processes?

References.

[1] Kaplan, Robert S. and David P. Norton, *The Balanced Scorecard*, Harvard Business School Press, 1996

[2] Ibid

[3] http://www.iveybusinessjournal.com/article.asp?intArticle_ID=527

[4] http://www.camagazine.com/index.cfm/ci_id/26179/la_id/1.htm

[5] Angel, Robert and Hubert Rampersad, 'Do Scorecards Add Up?', *CA Magazine*, May 2005

[6] Ittner, Christopher D., and David F. Larcker, 'Coming Up Short on Nonfinancial Performance Measurement,' *Harvard Business Review*, November 2003

[7] Gile, Keith and Connie Moore with Colin Teubner, 'Business Process Management (BPM) meets BI and Performance Management (xPM) Head On, Trends, Forrester Research, July 2005

Eight

An Integrated Approach

An organization's ability to learn, and translate that learning into action rapidly, is the ultimate competitive advantage.
— Jack Welch

By now it should be evident that any company dedicated to providing customers with "more for less" simply cannot afford to stand on its laurels. Successful, sustainable process improvement and management absolutely requires a consistent, replicable improvement method.

The importance of "methods" is usually acknowledged in the assessment of process management as a critical success factor. For example, a joint study between Babson College and The University of Queensland found that "methods," as defined by "the approaches and techniques that support and enable consistent process actions and outcomes," was one of six critical success factors in the assessment of the degree of process management maturity of an enterprise. The other five critical success factors in this study were identified as strategic alignment, governance, information technology, people, and culture.[1]

It is equally essential that the improvement and method be integrated with the company's governance structure, measurement approach, and information technology development.

Method is much more than a tool set. If it were simply a set of tools for improving business processes then it would simply be a commodity. A search of the Web reveals that. You can get a reengineering design toolkit, including templates, checklists, and guidelines, for the low price of $389.00 (including a binder and a CD-ROM). If Six Sigma Black Belt certification is what you are after, then on-line, distance-learning certification is available for as low as $995.00.

The effective deployment of an enterprise wide method necessarily involves the soft stuff as much as the hard stuff. The experience of both Caterpillar, Inc. and Xerox Corporation illustrates this.

Caterpillar Inc.

The decision to deploy 6 Sigma at Caterpillar Inc. dates back to the summer of 2000. Glen Barton, the then CEO and Chairman of Caterpillar, Inc., outlined the need for change at the firm's Strategic Review Conference in August 2000. He articulated a compelling vision of why change was needed even though Caterpillar was generally considered successful with one the world's most recognized brands. Barton pointed out that the firm's revenues had plateau-ed at $20 billion, and that warranty costs were increasing in spite of a long-standing focus on quality and reliability. He also stressed that for Caterpillar to remain competitive it would need to take at least 10% out of its cost base.

Barton proposed to the Caterpillar leadership team that the successful deployment of 6 Sigma can be instrumental in achieving the firm's goals of achieving $30 billion in sales by 2006, dramatically improving quality and reliability and thereby significantly improve customer satisfaction, and cutting costs by 10%. He invited Larry Bossidy of Allied Signal and Lou Giuliano of ITT Industries to address the leaders at the firm's Strategic Review Conference, and then asked for, and received, their support in deploying 6 Sigma on a global basis in 2001.

It takes time to ramp up the deployment of 6 Sigma in a firm as large and complex as Caterpillar. But by January 2001, the firm was ready to launch the effort. On December 19th, 2000, Glen Barton stood toe to toe with each of the company's 5 Group Presidents and 26 Vice Presidents and asked each in turn to express how they plan to support the new way of doing business with 6 Sigma.

There were a number of noteworthy factors in Caterpillar's deployment of 6 Sigma on a global basis. First, Glen Barton was a visible and vocal leader. He made it clear that he would "own" 6 Sigma, and took personal responsibility for its success. Next, he understood the importance of leadership. Barton stressed the so-called 3 C's – leadership with clarity, consistency, and commitment.

The firm's "recipe" for 6 Sigma success included three components. These were the 3 Cs (leading with clarity, consistency, and commitment), the seven Critical Success Factors of 6 Sigma and the goal of Six Sigma benefits exceeding costs in the first year of deployment (i.e., become accretive in 2001).[2]

Caterpillar invested heavily in 6 Sigma. It trained over 700 Black Belts representing 1% of the firm's employees, and 3500 Green Belts in 2001. It employed the services of not one, but three, consulting firms in training its employees; it retained control and made it crystal clear to each of the consulting firms that this is Caterpillar's initiative. It created the 6 Sigma Champion's Office (6SCO) led by Dave Burritt, the 6 Sigma Corporate Champion and supported by a small group of full time staff. Also a number of dedicated 6 Sigma Deployment Champions were established for each of Caterpillar's 26 autonomous operating divisions.

Caterpillar was accretive by the end of 2001. It achieved the goal of 6 Sigma benefits exceeding costs in the first year of deployment. Similar to the experience of other firms, much of the early benefits came from success in cost reduction. Yet, in 2001 it established global process ownership for certain key processes including Continuous Product Improvement (CPI) and Global Purchasing. In 2002, it launched global process ownerships and related initiatives for Order Fulfillment, New Product Introduction, and New Technology Introduction.

The results surpassed even Glen Barton's expectations by 2004. Revenues for the 2004 fiscal year surpassed $30 billion dollars, representing an increase of nearly $10 billion dollars since 2001. Profits rose to $2.035 billion by the end of 2004, representing an increase of over $1.2 billion since 2001.

In Caterpillar's 2004 Annual Report, an exuberant Barton wrote:

> I believe our people and world-class 6 Sigma deployment also distinguish Caterpillar from the crowd. What an incredible success story 6 Sigma has been for Caterpillar! It

is the way we do business — how we manage quality, eliminate waste, reduce costs, create new products and services, develop future leaders, and help the company grow profitably. We continue to find new ways to apply the methodology to tackle business challenges. Our leadership team is committed to encoding 6 Sigma into Caterpillar's "DNA" and extending its deployment to our dealers and suppliers — more than 500 of whom have already embraced the 6 Sigma way of doing business.

Together we are creating the industry's best supply chain, ready from top to bottom to meet the changing needs of those we serve.

What contributed to Caterpillar's success? There were several key factors, to a large extent in line with the firm's critical success factors (CSFs) for 6 Sigma:

- *Top down, committed leadership* was needed. With 26 autonomous businesses spread around the globe, reliance on a bottom-up deployment strategy would have been disastrous.
- *Constantly articulated and reinforced clear goals and expectations* was another part of the puzzle. Caterpillar used multiple media to do this including a series of three internal publications called "Giant Steps."
- *A significant investment in 6 Sigma* training and deployment support also played a key role.
- *An aligned incentive system* whereby up to 20% of individual incentive compensation was based on 6 Sigma performance was instrumental. This included overcoming union objections — no small feat in itself.
- *Finally, a process framework and mindset* in deploying 6 Sigma led to some of the biggest gains. Caterpillar employed not only the DMAIC methodology, but also the DMEDI approach to attack larger cross-functional processes.

That's not to say that there weren't some serious challenges along the way, some of which persist to this day.

In a July 2004 phone conversation with Dave Burritt, the 6

Sigma Corporate Champion in 2001 and 2002 and currently the firm's Chief Financial Officer, Burritt said:

> I think we've made some very good progress in embracing process thinking – but by no stretch could I say that we are there yet. With CPI – continuous product improvement – we've had a lot of success – also on global purchasing and on the innovation side …our breakthrough engine technology…we've been able to apply 6 Sigma. But in other areas, we've had less success, in applying globally reaching (processes), with common approaches.

Also, Caterpillar, like many other firms who have deployed 6 Sigma, continues to struggle with the role of the Process Owner. This is just as much a shortcoming of the 6 Sigma method itself, as it is an implementation issue. In 6 Sigma, the Role of the Process Owner is not well defined. Generally, the Process Owner takes over from the Black Belt in the "control" phase of the DMAIC method. This hand-off in itself is problematic. There is scant guidance on whether the Process Owner role is global, local, and at what management level. In practice, it's all over the map. Caterpillar has defined various levels of process ownership including:

1. Owner: Personally accountable

2. Facilitator: Influence but not accountable

3. Architect: Establish and track targets

4. Scorekeeper: Track and report

5. Cheerleader: Provide periodic updates

To Caterpillar's credit, they have not taken a "one size fits all" approach to Six Sigma. Instead, they have built something that is tailor made for Caterpillar. Granted, Caterpillar began its journey with a singular focus on deploying its 6 Sigma program. Yet, the Caterpillar Inc. example is an illustration of the importance of employing a tailor made method with a keen attention to governance, measurement, and company culture.

The case of Xerox Corporation is equally instructive.

Xerox Corporation

The origin of Xerox Lean Six Sigma can be traced back to Xerox's initial "Leadership through Quality" initiative in the early 1980s. Xerox had a long history of deploying improvement tools and techniques across the corporation, centered on improving process performance to create higher levels of customer satisfaction, quality, and productivity.

In 2002, Xerox faced increasing competition, and its share price was under pressure. Anne Mulcahy, Xerox's CEO, was committed to "returning Xerox to greatness."

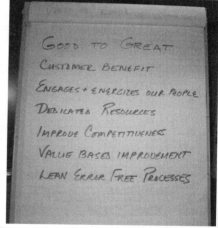

Why Xerox Lean Six Sigma?

Leadership Committee
November 22, 2002

What I worry most about is how to return Xerox to greatness...

Lean Six Sigma is not the only answer, but it's a significant part of the equation.

Lean Six Sigma is incredibly different...

-- Anne Mulcahy

GOOD TO GREAT
CUSTOMER BENEFIT
ENGAGES + ENERGIZES OUR PEOPLE
DEDICATED RESOURCES
IMPROVE COMPETITIVENESS
VALUE BASED IMPROVEMENT
LEAN ERROR FREE PROCESSES

Figure 8.1. Why Xerox Lean Six Sigma?[3]

She believed that a customer centric approach based on adopting a global Lean Six Sigma effort was an important part of the solution. Figure 8.1 depicts the flip chart page from the November 22, 2002, leadership committee meeting and Mulcahy's key comments.

At Xerox, Lean Six Sigma is viewed in three dimensions: Projects and Results, Cultural Change, and Leadership Development.

It was recognized early on that to assure continued progress the firm must balance all three of these critical dimensions.

George Maszle, Director Lean Six Sigma, stated at a March 2004 ASQRS conference, "While the economic benefits from the hundreds of Lean Six Sigma projects will positively impact financial results, a failure to change our culture or develop our Black Belts into future leaders may mean that the business results will be short lived."

Xerox took an aggressive approach to deploying Lean Six Sigma globally. Its path to transforming the way the firm worked included the following key components:

- Projects selected based on value creation opportunities
- Consistent financial results tracking approach
- Deploy and train resources in roles as defined (Full Time Black Belts, Full Time Deployment Managers, Sponsors, Green Belts)
- Assign demonstrated top performers to the full-time roles
- Define organizational structure to enable success
- Engagement of operations leadership and integration of Lean Six Sigma into "How we run daily business operations"
- Achieve critical mass toward the Xerox transformation of at least 0.5% of the employee population as Black Belts in 2003 and another 0.5% in 2004.

Xerox's Mulcahy believed that leadership makes a significant difference. It's not just talk – she is reported to personally own the "quote to cash" process for North America and to monitor process performance. In addition to having leaders such as Mulcahy communicate progress via speeches, meetings, and newsletters, Xerox has also established an extensive intranet site that provides reference information, deployment details, project successes, and answers to frequently asked questions. Formal training also plays a key role in preparing all employees to actively participate in the Lean Six Sigma effort.

Xerox prides itself on an integrated approach to process improvement, where the customer is at the center of what the firm does, and the firm integrates customer focus with clear linkages to business strategies and objectives. This is illustrated by the key messages that underpin the Xerox integrated strategy in its application of Lean Six Sigma:[4]

- Integrates customer focus with clear linkage to business strategy and objectives

- Customer at center of all we do

- Builds on quality legacy with full arsenal of industry proven Lean & Six Sigma processes & tools

- Supported by infrastructure, resource commitment, and project discipline to focus on key business issues and critical to customer opportunities.

As a result of this integrated approach, Xerox appears to increasingly employ methods other than the standard DMAIC approach (Define, Measure, Analyze, Improve, and Control). It has developed a structured approach to decide upon the improvement method to be used, depending upon whether the focus is on product or process, and then, whether it is new or existing. Three principal methodologies are deployed as shown on Figure 8.2 below: the IDOV (Identify, Design, Optimize, Verify) for new product development, the DMAIC approach for existing product or process improvement, and the DMEDI model (Define, Measure, Explore, Develop, Implement) for new process development.

Granted, the success of Xerox Corporation and Caterpillar Inc. is in part predicated upon some of the characteristics introduced in Chapter 3, including a long history of process improvement, a keen focus on customer satisfaction, a CEO with commitment to the potential role of process improvement and management in creating value for both customers and shareholders, concern for the challenge of growth or an imminent competitive threat, and a certain degree of cultural fit. However, their journey towards an integrated method of improvement is a fundamental part of their story.

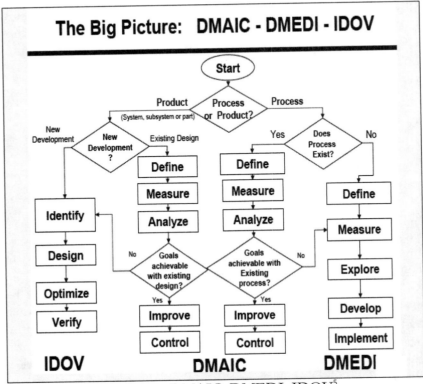

Figure 8.2. DMAIC, DMEDI, IDOV[5]

What About Six Sigma?

Six Sigma is currently the most popular method of process improvement. It has been observed that nearly 50% of companies reported the use of Six Sigma or Lean Six Sigma in their organizations. It continues to be in widespread use. A long list of companies such as General Electric, Bank of America, Dow Chemical, Caterpillar, Honeywell, Motorola, DuPont, 3M, Xerox, and many others have used it to improve business performance and realize millions of dollars in bottom-line savings.[6]

Six Sigma has a lot to offer. First, there are the success stories provided by visible advocates such as Jack Welch at G.E. and Larry Bossidy at Allied Signal. Next, it has a robust, albeit almost cookie-cutter training method, which specifies a number of useful parameters – including management roles, and the number of black belts to be trained – and provides helpful guidance on project scope, duration, and expected benefits. This is clearly attractive and useful in terms of rolling it out. Then, there is the battery of statistical tools integral to the methodology.

Both Caterpillar and Xerox used a variation of Six Sigma to launch their process improvement and management efforts. So, why not use Six Sigma as the principle methodology to implement process management across the enterprise?

That's a commonly asked question. In theory the answer would appear to be a resounding – Yes. However, in practice, the deployment of Six Sigma has a number of shortcomings that must be addressed by a firm if it wishes to successfully use Six Sigma as the launching pad for their process improvement program.

Before addressing these, let's first explore some of the strengths of Six Sigma. Many leaders today are attracted to the rigor of the method and the large array of statistical tools in Six Sigma.

While there are virtually dozens of tools in the Six Sigma tool kit which generally rely on identifying critical-to-customer requirements, the most frequently applied, as cited by Hoerl and Snee, tend to be:[7]

- Process mapping
- Cause-and-effect matrix
- Measurement system analysis
- Capability study
- Failure modes and effects analysis (FMEA)
- Multi-vari study
- Design of experiments
- Control plans

The emphasis on the voice of the customer (VOC) and the focus on defect reduction are also major strengths of the Six Sigma approach.

Although the DMAIC model (Define, Measure, Analyze, Improve, Control) is the best-known Six Sigma improvement method, there is increasing use of more radical improvement approaches in the DFSS (Design for Six Sigma) arsenal. These include the DMADV (Define, Measure, Analyze, Design and Verify) and the DMEDI (Define, Measure, Explore, Develop, Implement) methodologies, both of which are meant to design a process based on customer requirements.

But Six Sigma is not without its critics. As far back as 1998, Del Jones, in a USA Today article, quoted critics who claimed that "It's really Statistical Process Control in new clothing," and it "will eventually go the way of other fads, but probably not until Welch and Bossidy retire." Of course, both Welch and Bossidy have since retired – but Six Sigma is still going strong.

The fact is that in theory Six Sigma is a robust process improvement and management methodology. In theory, it has the potential to be the principal method in a firm's overarching process management approach. Of course, this requires that it be launched by leadership with passion, focusing the organization outward on meeting the needs of customers.

There is ample guidance in the literature on precisely how to do this. In *Strategic Six Sigma: Best Practices from the Executive Suite,* the authors provide valuable insight on the following key steps that make strategic Six Sigma efforts successful[8]

1. Build a committed leadership team.

2. Integrate Strategic Six Sigma principles into the company's strategy planning and deployment processes.

3. Ensure that the company is passionate about obtaining customer requirements.

4. Design, organize, and run the business using a process framework.

5. Develop quantifiable measures – then demand tangible results from people.

6. Establish incentives, create accountability, reward performance.

7. Recognize that success with Six Sigma means making a full-time commitment and applying the manpower to ensure that Six Sigma projects succeed.

Yet, in practice, Six Sigma can have some very serious short-comings including, but not limited to, the following:

- It is often deployed as the means to cut costs.
- It is frequently deployed solely on a functional basis.
- It promotes the use of many small projects and lacks an effective mechanism to roll up or integrate these small projects into a larger, enterprise wide improvement plan.
- Projects often rely heavily on the Black Belt.
- The linkage to and use of enabling technology is often sub-optimal.

In order to use Six Sigma effectively as the basis for company wide process improvement and management, it's important to recognize and avoid these pitfalls.

What's the Objective:
Customer Satisfaction or Cost Cutting?

In theory, Six Sigma should be deployed to meet customer needs and strategic improvement objectives. In theory, it is focused first and foremost on improving the customer experience through defect reduction.

In practice, Six Sigma is often deployed as the means to cut costs, even though lip service is paid to improving the customer experience. For example, in one Six Sigma training program rolled out in a billion dollar company, it was noted that the customer was not mentioned until page 37, and then not again until page 127, in the training program documentation.[9]

Maybe it's all right to deploy Six Sigma in order to cut costs as long as the firm's critical business issue is cost reduction and there is the intent to go beyond cost cutting to a broader range of objectives in the future.

However, in practice, a surprising number of firms simply do not get beyond the phase of deploying Six Sigma for cost containment and never reach the true potential as articulated by Jack Welch: "At Six Sigma's core is an idea that can turn a company inside out, focusing the organization outward on the customer."[10]

The traditional mindset of leaders is the primary culprit in this regard. Many executives think in terms of dollars – not in terms of the processes that create value for customers. Even Jack Welch, arguably the most influential early advocate of Six Sigma, reported "We were three years into Six Sigma before we got it."[11]

What Welch meant was that for three years GE measured improvements based on an average. In other words, the focus was on improving things like the average cycle time for delivering orders. And they celebrated these improvements – even though it had little to do with what customers really wanted, which was to get what they ordered, when they asked for it. Now, the concept of providing customers with what they ordered and when they asked that it be delivered is certainly not new. It's been around for at least 40 years, if not more, as a fundamental underlying principle of quality and process improvement movements. So why did it take GE three years to get it? Part of the answer may be related to the next practical challenge with Six Sigma, that it is often deployed on a functional or departmental basis.

Six Sigma is often deployed with a functional/departmental bias

In theory, Six Sigma stresses the importance of both a customer and a process focus. Smith and Blakeslee have found that "organizations that identify improvement projects, not as isolated endeavors, but as strategic improvement activities within a company's business process framework will achieve a faster ROI."[12] These authors outline in some detail the theory on how firms can align Six Sigma improvement initiatives to core processes and key performance indicators.

Often, this does not occur in practice. In practice, Six Sigma is frequently deployed along functional or departmental lines simply because that is the predominant mental model of leadership. Even when the intent is to view the business in a process context, the traditional view of how the firm is organized can strongly influence the alleged process view.

Whenever Six Sigma is deployed on a departmental basis, it is observed that black belts are trained and assigned to the functional departments. They are then typically tasked with completing 4-6 projects per annum, where each project delivers around $250,000.00 of cost savings. In other words, while the rhetoric may emphasize customer centricity, the action is focused on cost reduction.

This method of deployment understandably leads to a large number of relatively small projects, which in turn drives a certain degree of duplication of effort.

A further factor in this respect is a mental model bias in the Six Sigma methodology to avoid tackling large cross, functional processes. "We're not here to solve world hunger" is a common phrase used to justify avoiding large cross-functional projects. Even in those instances where large, end-to-end processes are addressed, the common practice is to look at these at the Define phase and then quickly move to launch many DMAIC projects within the boundaries of the large process to carry out the actual improvement and management of small parts of the process.

One firm, known for its success in deploying Six Sigma, reported that it had over 1,500 active projects in an effort to improve the firm's order fulfillment process. Not only does such an approach produce a certain amount of redundant activity, but, also, the task of rolling up project insights and cross-geographic integration becomes problematic.

Given the predominant practice of launching many smaller projects, it is not surprising that most projects are not very cross-functional in nature. Accordingly, some of the largest opportunities for improvement, which have to do with managing cross-functional hand-offs in a different and novel way, are not addressed.

There are two key points to note here. First, as some of the largest opportunities for improvement are found at cross-functional handoffs, the firm that fails to tackle the end-to-end, cross-functional processes, sub-optimizes the opportunity for perform-ance improvement. Next, whenever hundreds of small Six Sigma projects are launched to fix the problems in one large process, there is a need for an overarching process framework to integrate results and exercise control. In the absence of such a framework, the longer-term benefits of the improvements can be compromised.

A related point that adversely impacts the deployment of Six Sigma in practice is the role of the Black Belt and the Project Champion.

Heavy reliance on the Black Belt

In theory, Six Sigma has well defined roles for Project Cham-pions, Black Belts, Green Belts, and so on. In practice, when it comes to actual projects, there is a very high degree of reliance on the Black Belt.

In theory the Project Champion, typically a member of the leadership team, has the following responsibilities:
- Guide and assist in the selection of projects
- Lead (along with the black belt) in drafting the initial project charter
- Engaging "stakeholders" to participate in project reviews
- Obtaining Black Belts and other resources needed to conduct the project
- Removing obstacles to the successful completion of the project
- Chairing regular progress reviews

This role is well suited for the smaller projects within the con-text of one department. However, a commonly expressed concern is the difficulty of finding a strong Project Champion. In those in-stances where cross-functional processes are identified for im-provement, the Six Sigma approach suffers from failing to suffi-ciently engage the peers of the Project Champion. While the Project

Champion and the black belt have joint responsibility for identifying so-called stakeholders and engaging them in the project, the practical deployment of the methodology is not strong in terms of the role of an "Executive Committee" or "Steering Team," meaning a group of senior leaders from the various departments touched by the process in question who would act collaboratively to guide the project and make decisions.

The term "stakeholder" is generally interpreted as a party that has an interest in an organization. For example, the typical stakeholders of a company include stockholders, bondholders, customers, suppliers, employees, etc. In the context of a Six Sigma project, stakeholders are those people who have an interest in the results of the project. In practical terms, having interest in the project is simply not enough when it comes to larger, cross-functional projects.

The absence of a true "Executive Committee" or "Steering Team" has repercussions in several areas. First, it can adversely affect the definition of the project by failing to include assessment of certain touching processes. Next, and arguably most importantly, in the absence of a strong Project Champion, heavy reliance on the Black Belt can lead to challenges in obtaining the right resources and deployment of those resources on the project. This can lead to the use of part-time resources, when in fact the project scope and complexity actually calls for the use of full time resources. Further, it can lead to unproductive project meeting schedules where resources are made available only for a few hours a week, thereby extending project cycle times and even compromising project success. Then, in the absence of the type of senior level collaboration typical to Steering Teams, reliance on the Black Belt can lead to challenges in overcoming obstacles, particularly in the phases of improve and control. A connected issue is the relationship, or lack thereof, between Six Sigma leadership and information technology.

Sub-optimal linkage and use of enabling technology

In theory, Six Sigma should facilitate the work of people in the information systems area. In practice, the linkage and use of IT is frequently sub-optimal.

A recent posting in the "Ask the Expert" forum, on www.cio.com, provides an interesting perspective.

The topic had to do with the use of Business Process Management (BPM) software and Six Sigma. In this case, the expert was Rashid Khan, CEO and founder of Ultimus, a global business process management software company. Khan's statement is representative of what many in the IT area believe. He wrote,

> "Six Sigma has some relationship with BPM but not as much as it is hyped to be. A good understanding of Six Sigma enables a person to better analyze and understand their processes, and this has a direct benefit for BPM. However, the vast majority of processes that are automated using BPM do not require the depth of up-front analysis that occurs in a Six Sigma-type methodology. In these cases Six Sigma is likely to become a distraction rather than a real benefit."[13]

The apparent lack of alignment with enabling technology is somewhat puzzling as one might think that there would be significant synergy in this respect. Once again, it may be a mindset and a structural issue. IT professionals tend to think in terms of applications and Six Sigma professionals tend to think in terms of statistics and variance.

Why is there such a significant gap between theory and practice? There are three major reasons that apply to Six Sigma or, for that matter, to any other process improvement method:

- There is a problem whenever any method is perceived as the "end" instead of as the "means." Maybe it's all right to begin that way, but a true integrated method will evolve beyond that quickly.

- The absence of governance at the enterprise level is problematic. Whenever process ownership is limited to the sub-process level, the longer-term sustainability of the approach becomes compromised.

- In the twenty-first century, the close integration of any broad based improvement method and information technology is a fundamental requirement.

The organizations that find a way to bridge the gap between theory and practice will find that Six Sigma remains a robust, powerful improvement method. As outlined in the Caterpillar and Xerox examples, it can form the foundation for a company-wide program and lead to even more powerful, integrated methods.

The Benefits of an Integrated Approach

Several subject matter experts have advocated an integrated approach to process improvement and management. Dr. Tom Davenport presented preliminary research on the merits of an integrated approach or what he called a "Hybrid Process Improvement Methodology" at Babson College's Process Management Research Center conference on June 1, 2005. Davenport discussed the merits of a comprehensive or "hybrid" approach to process improvement and management. He identified the evolution of various approaches and reviewed some case examples of companies such as Johnson & Johnson, Horizon Blue Cross/Blue Shield of NJ, Air Products, and Teradyne, which are moving along a continuum from relying on just one method to deploying multiple tools without an overall method. The conclusions of Babson College's research on this topic included the following key points:

- As organizations become more sophisticated and skilled in process management, there appears to be a movement in the direction of a hybrid approach.
- Such an approach is probably not right for everyone; it requires very high levels of executive support and investment in employee training.
- While a particular method may be a good way to begin with process management, hybridization appears to assist in the effort to continue with process management.
- Hybrid methods not only facilitate process management, but also indicate that other things are going well.[14]

Table 8.1 summarizes what constitutes an integrated approach and its benefits.

Features	Benefits
▪ The method is the means and not the end ▪ Top down governance structure ▪ Method is comprised of various tool sets ▪ The scope and nature of the project drives tool selection ▪ Tight linkage to information technology	▪ Focus on customer value creation ▪ Increased chance of sustainability ▪ Greater flexibility ▪ Avoids the pitfall of trying to solve all problems the same way ▪ Can rapidly take advantage of technology advances

Table 8.1. Features and Benefits of an Integrated Approach

Schlegel and Smith also advocate the benefits of an integrated approach to improvement.[15] They see it as the next step of evolution in supply-chain management and propose that an integrated approach, where the focus is on strategic priorities and a set of tools are deployed to obtain the desired results, can take organizations to a new plane of operational performance. Their research cites companies such as Dow where it is observed that coupling a more integrated focus on process improvement with a supply chain strategy and ERP implementation would have accelerated benefits.[16]

How will you know when you're making progress in deploying an integrated improvement method? See Table 8.2 below.

What's Needed:
Deploy an Integrated Improvement Method to Sustain Focus
Signs of Progress:
▪ An increasing percent of the workforce is trained on a range of process improvement tools ▪ Process owners play a visible role in process improvement and management education ▪ There is increasing recognition that the method of process improvement is the means and not the end ▪ Leaders relentlessly communicate the central role of improving

> and managing business processes in performing for customers
> - Company culture has fully incorporated the recognition of people and teams who were instrumental in improving performance for customers

Table 8.2. Signs of Progress

As companies progress in the use of an integrated set of process improvement methods they will naturally see tool sets as the means for obtaining improvements and creating greater value for customers and shareholders as the end. However, to do that successfully requires a more confident and mature leadership team to deal with the inherent complexity of proper tool selection and the associated multi-faceted training requirements.

Chapter 8: Self-Assessment Questions:

1. Do you see process improvement tool sets as the "end" or as the "means" in improving business performance?
2. Are your process improvement initiatives closely linked to strategy?
3. Is there an enterprise view of improvement initiatives, with clarity around the size of the gap to be closed for the company's critical business processes?
4. Does your leadership team determine the type and scope of needed improvement prior to deciding which tool sets need to be deployed?
5. Are customer requirements front and center in driving the selection of process improvements?
6. Are IT enablers closely coupled to the use of improvement methods such as Six Sigma, Lean, and reengineering?
7. Has your organization invested sufficiently in education on various tools sets and their optimal deployment?
8. Is there a mechanism in place to review and refine the set of process improvement tools after each major project?

References.

[1] De Bruin, Tonia, Process Management Maturity: Executive Summary, September, 2005

[2] The seven critical success factors of 6 Sigma at Caterpillar, Inc., were based on principles outlined in Smith and Blakeslee's *Strategic Six Sigma; Best Practices from the Executive Suite*

[3] Maszle, George, ASQRS Conference Presentation, March 2004

[4] Maszle, George, ASQRS Conference Presentation, March 2004

[5] Provided by George Maszle, Xerox Corporation

[6] Hoerl, Roger, and Ronald Snee, A Holistic View of Six Sigma, *Inform IT*, December 4, 2004

[7] Hoerl, Roger, and Ronald Snee, A Holistic View of Six Sigma, *Inform IT*, December 4, 2004

[8] Smith, Dick and Jerry Blakeslee with Richard Koonce, *Strategic Six Sigma; Best Practices from the Executive Suite, Wiley, 2002*

[9] Goodman, John and Jon Theuerkauf, What's Wrong with Six Sigma, *Quality Progress*, Vol 38, No. 1, January 2005

[10] Welch, Jack with John A. Byrne, *Straight from the Gut*, Warner Business Books, 2001, page 330

[11] Ibid, page 337

[12] Smith, Dick and Jerry Blakeslee with Richard Koonce, *Strategic Six Sigma; Best Practices from the Executive Suite*, Wiley, 2002

[13] http://www.cio.com/ posted on April 11, 2005

[14] Based on presentations at the Babson College Process Management Research Center, June 2005

[15] Schlegel, Gregory L., and Richard C. Smith, 'The Next Stage of Supply Chain Excellence', *Supply Chain Management Review*, March 1, 2005

[16] Ibid

Nine

The Search for
Competitive Advantage

Competitive advantage is at the heart of a firm's performance in competitive markets. After several decades of vigorous expansion and prosperity, however, many firms lost sight of competitive advantage in their scramble for growth and pursuit of diversification. Today the importance of competitive advantage could hardly be greater. Firms throughout the world face slower growth as well as domestic and global competitors that are no longer acting as if the expanding pie were big enough for all.
— Michael Porter

That is how the search for competitive advantage may have been launched in 1985 by Dr. Michael Porter in his landmark book *Competitive Advantage.*

Even though the term "competitive advantage" has eluded rigorous definition, a wide-ranging discussion of what constitutes competitive advantage has taken place since 1985.

Indeed, it seems that recently we are obsessed with competitive advantage. In addition to Porter's prolific writing on this topic, others have written about:

- Advancing corporate governance from compliance to competitive advantage[1]
- How taking the high road creates a competitive advantage[2]
- Crafting and executing strategy in the quest for competitive advantage[3]
- How global leaders use information for growth and competitive advantage[4]

What is competitive advantage? What role does process management have when it comes to competitive advantage? To what extent is this new? What's needed for organizations to deploy process management in search of competitive advantage? It is these questions that this final chapter will explore.

What is Competitive Advantage?

Competitive advantage is the phenomenon of creating more customer value than competitors do. It occurs when a company creates the capability of attracting and retaining customers by providing them with "more for less" on a sustainable basis.

If you thought competitive advantage was about profits, think again. Customer value creation is the objective; corporate profits are simply a means of keeping score.

That's not to say that keeping score isn't important. It is! It's the only way of measuring the company's ability to attract and satisfy customers on an enduring basis. That's why two of the recent studies on what constitutes sustained business success, and hence competitive advantage, rely on quantitative measurement of profitability, be it total return to shareholders (TRS) or cumulative stock market returns. The studies in question are: "Good to Great"[5] and "What Really Works."[6] Both of these two studies are based on substantive research and quantitative analysis.

What Really Works	Good to Great
Research Basis: Ten year study (1986-1996) which examined the performance of 160 companies in terms of the correlation between "total return to shareholders" (TRS) and management practices.	Research Basis: Began with a list of 1,435 companies, pared down to 126 companies. Then, identified "great companies" as those which have generated cumulative stock returns that beat the general stock market by at least 300 percent over a 15-year period. Included a comparison of the good-to-great firms to a control group of companies to discover the seven essential factors that separate the good-to-great firms from the merely good ones.

The Four plus Two formula: All four of the primary practices and two of the secondary practices. The primary practices: 1. Devise a clearly stated, focused strategy. 2. Develop flawless operational execution. 3. Create a performance-oriented culture. 4. Build a fast, flexible, flat company structure. The secondary practices: 1. Hold on to people who show talent and find more of them. 2. Keep leadership committed to the business. 3. Develop innovations that transform your industry. 4. Make growth happen with mergers, acquisitions, and partnerships.	The seven essential factors that separate the good-to-great firms from the merely good ones are: 1. "Level 5" Leaders. These CEOs put their companies ahead of their own egos. 2. A Focus on Who Before What. Leaders concentrated on getting the right people in place before pursuing a new vision or strategy. 3. A Willingness to Confront the Brutal Truth. Every good-to-great company acknowledged difficulties, yet believed it would win in the end. 4. The Hedgehog Concept. If you cannot be the best in the world at your core competence, it cannot form the basis of a great company. 5. A Culture of Discipline. When you have disciplined people, you don't need a hierarchy, a bureaucracy, or excessive controls. 6. Technology Accelerators. Good-to-great companies did not use technology to ignite a transformation, but they did find new uses for widely available technology. 7. The Flywheel and the Doom Loop. Momentum for greatness is built slowly, rather than in a single, grand initiative.

Table 9.1. Key Factors that Contribute to
Sustained Business Success

What story does this summary tell? The right CEO, a focus on "who" as well as "what," and an appreciation for the importance of "talent" are just a few of the critical factors. And there is no substitute for passion.

Tellingly, neither study explicitly mentioned process management. Yet, a customer-centric, process view of the world is a part, and an important part, of the mix. So, let's consider the role of the enterprise level process view as it relates to the above-cited management practices.

The Role of Process Management

A customer centric, process view of the business enables the development of a clearly stated, focused strategy in two ways. First, measuring a company's current performance in satisfying customer requirements with respect to the quality, timeliness, completeness, and responsiveness as part of its "environmental scan," a company will be able to realistically assess where it stands in terms of providing customers with "more for less." Then, an enterprise process perspective enables the firm to articulate which of its large business processes needs to be improved by how much in order to deliver on its strategy. In so doing, not only is it possible to achieve a more lucid roadmap for key strategic initiatives, but the company also sets the stage to confront the brutal facts in terms of the size of the performance gap to be bridged.

A process improvement approach is an essential component of developing flawless operational execution. The more sophisticated firms will not launch a single, grand initiative. Instead, they will demonstrate strong executive support and invest in broad based education in order to take best advantage of the benefits of an integrated approach to improvement. They will focus unrelentingly on strategic priorities and deploy an integrated set of improvement tools to take their organizations to a new level of operational performance.

The role of this process view at the enterprise level, when combined with a more balanced perspective on measurement, and aligned recognition and reward systems can significantly contribute to a performance-oriented culture, where performing for customers trumps hierarchy, bureaucracy, and excessive controls.

The process view of business is also a key enabler of leadership. It facilitates knowing the business, and understanding the work, the roles of key departments, and key people in the whole workflow as it crosses traditional organizational boundaries. Executives become better equipped to insist on realism by looking at the business from the customer's point of view and measuring performance in terms of the timeliness, quality, and cost of products and services provided to customers. The business process view assists executives in setting clear, realistic goals and priorities in terms of the value created for customers and shareholders, and also by expressing priorities in this way it facilitates acknowledging the people from different departments who make significant contributions in observable, measurable terms.

By viewing the role of information technology (IT) as fundamental to enabling the performance of an organization's business processes to create value for customers and shareholders, companies can avoid attempting to use technology to ignite transformation. They can, on the other hand, effectively deploy new applications of widely available technology to make it easier for employees to serve the needs of customers.

A process view of the business is essential to the effective integration of mergers and acquisitions. Of course, there's much more to successful mergers than just a process view. The strong alignment among key members of management on what needs to be done, avoiding the pitfall of premature cost cutting, and the dedication to letting people know whether they have a job in the new entity are also some of the critical success factors. But process does play a big part, especially in a successful integration.

Where do people fit into this equation? Front and center! People are the company, for as John Seely Brown, former Chief Scientist for Xerox, pointed out, "Processes don't do work, people do"?[7]

To What Extent Are These Concepts New?

Are these concepts new? If considered one by one, not exactly. When considered in their entirety, absolutely. It's not just in the academic world that there's a long lead-time between concept development and practical application. As far back as the early 1990s, pioneers such as Dr. Tom Davenport, Dr. Geary Rummler, and

Alan Brache, advocated that business must not be viewed just in terms of functions, divisions, products, but also in terms of business processes.

They outlined that process improvement and/or innovation has enormous potential for helping any organization achieve major reductions in process cost or time, and major improvements in quality, flexibility, responsiveness, and other business objectives.

They reinforced that unless leaders can agree on the way work should be planned, performed, and measured, it will be very difficult to systematically improve performance or effect innovation. They stressed that information technology will not be effective without simultaneously addressing aspects of human performance.

They emphasized that taking a process approach implies adopting the customer's point of view. That's how value is created for customers. That's why customers should be represented in all phases of a process management approach, and, while you can't measure or improve hierarchical structure in any absolute sense, processes have cost, time, output quality, and customer satisfaction that you can measure and improve. They wrote about the need for processes to have owners, and proposed that process ownership can be seen as an additional or alternative dimension of the formal organizational structure that during periods of radical change take precedence over other dimensions of structure.

They outlined that a process perspective implies a horizontal view of the business – and involves de-emphasizing the functional structure of the firm. Around the same time, others were predicting the rise of the "horizontal corporation" where hierarchy and departmental boundaries would largely be eliminated, and corporations would chose to organize according to multi-disciplinary teams that perform core processes.[8]

Although a number of firms have embraced the principles of managing business processes, it is somewhat puzzling why these have not been more widely adopted.

There are several reasons. First, much of the literature on the topic was unduly mechanistic. Next, the link to leadership mindset and behavior has not been well articulated. The purpose of this book has been to address this gap. To date, there has not been a strong enough, compelling reason to change. The events of the past few years and the next few years are likely to change all that.

What Does the Future Hold?

What's needed for organizations to deploy process management for competitive advantage? It has to start with a shift in conventional wisdom and different leadership mindset and behavior. What that involves is depicted in Table 9.2. How important is this? About 50 to 70 percent of how employees perceive their organization's climate can be traced to the actions of the leader.[9]

Leadership Mindset	Leadership Behavior
▪ Think systemically. Imagine. Collaborate. ▪ Be childlike. Ask "why?" "What if?" ▪ Trust middle-management teams; they are closer to the way work is done. ▪ Believe in the value of measuring and rewarding performing for customers. ▪ Understand that technology is available to all; it's how you apply it that counts. ▪ Appreciate that what gets measured gets done and what gets rewarded gets done consistently. ▪ Know that language, tools and decision-making are primary determinants of culture.	▪ Develop an enterprise view on performing for customers. ▪ Design business processes to deliver on business goals. ▪ Assure that organization design, as defined by structure, measures, and rewards, enables the organization to perform for customers. ▪ Deploy enabling information technology to enhance the performance of the firm's processes. ▪ Tightly link a customer centric performance measurement system to budgets and operating reviews. ▪ Develop and deploy integrated tools to sustain customer value creation.

Table 9.2. A Summary of Leadership Mindset and Behavior

While leadership mindset and behavior is where process management starts, it's not where it ends. To fully realize the power of process management you must engage the entire organization in performing for customers.

That requires making progress in measuring what matters to customers and assuring accountability for the performance of the company's large, cross-functional business processes. Most progressive companies conduct customer satisfaction and employee satisfaction surveys. These can be valuable, but they are not enough.

The company-wide deployment of process concepts needs to be led by leaders and embraced by employees. How will you know when this is happening? You will see a significantly higher level of interdepartmental connectedness and a commensurate reduction in the degree of interdepartmental conflict. You will feel a higher level of "esprit de corps."

How important is this? Extremely! According to Dr. Kevin McCormack, there is a strong correlation between companies' overall business performance and measures of business process orientation. Companies with strong measures of business process orientation tend to have better "esprit de corps," better connectedness, and less interdepartmental conflict.[10]

McCormack has developed a survey instrument that can be used not only to assess employees' perceptions on process jobs, process management and measurement systems, interdepartmental connectedness, and interdepartmental conflict, but also to correlate employee perception on these topics to their views on overall business performance.[11] The BPO survey instrument is contained in Appendix 2. Isn't it about time that you began to assess employees' perceptions on these issues?

What else is needed? From an external perspective, maybe it's time that Wall Street analysts stopped focusing primarily on publicly traded companies' guidance for the next quarter and began to ask questions to explore how the company is actually performing for customers.

Similarly, more focus on this topic by members of the company's Board of Directors would help. This may have already begun according to a survey in The McKinsey Quarterly on Forbes.com where it was reported that

A full 70% of the directors want to know more about customers, competitors, suppliers, the likes and dislikes of consumers, market share, brand strength, levels of satisfaction with products, and so on. And upward of half want to know more about the state of the organization, including the skills and capabilities needed to realize the corporate business strategy, both now and in the future.[12]

Also, the primary technology vendors have an important potential role to play in emphasizing an enterprise view of performance and not just the tools. This would help business leaders come to terms with the rapid proliferation of innovative technology and how to best apply technology to improve operational performance.

From an internal perspective, leaders need to appreciate the power of the process perspective as a new dimension of management and as the means to maintain and sustain an enduring focus on performing for customers. Leaders are clear on the need to manage businesses, functions, and products or brands. The talent to manage a company's business end-to-end processes in a value chain context represents the fourth dimension of management.

Similarly, leaders need to recognize that process management provides the means to leverage the organization's capabilities. Capabilities can easily be defined in terms of cross-functional processes, and the measurement and governance of these capabilities provides the potential for significant leverage. Remember Michael Porter's words, "Activities, then, are the basics of competitive advantage. Overall advantage or disadvantage results from all of a company's activities, not only a few."[13]

When will these needed changes take place? Some are already beginning to happen and will pick up pace sooner and faster than you might think. Process management is no substitute for great products and services. Process management cannot be effectively deployed in the absence of leadership talent and management discipline. However, given the fundamentals of a good organization, it has the power to tear down the walls of internal fiefdoms, leverage organizational capability, and engage the entire organization in performing for customers.

Only a small percent of organizations will decide to embark on such a journey, given the entrenched nature of traditional, functional thinking. Even fewer will succeed. But that's the nature of competition, isn't it?

Geico Insurance ran an amusing advertisement on television. An executive is speaking at a staff meeting. He says, "Our task is to make accounts payable exciting again." As he speaks, one of the young men on the staff is making faces and silly hand gestures, mocking the speaker. Then the speaker notices the young man.

The ad voice continues. "In the time it takes to clean out your desk, you can save hundreds with Geico."

Maybe leaders will soon recognize that their task is to make the work of delivering "more for less" exciting again. If not, a lot of desks may have to be cleaned out. Do you feel compelled to act? Now is the time to decide.

References.

[1] Charan, Ram, *Boards that Deliver: Advancing Corporate Governance from Compliance to Competitive Advantage,* Jossey-Bass, 2005

[2] Telford, Dana and Adrian Gostick, *The Integrity Advantage: How Taking the High Road Creates a Competitive Advantage in Business,* Gibbs Smith, 2003

[3] Thompson, Arthur A., Jr. et al, *Crafting and Executing Strategy : The Quest for Competitive Advantage,* McGraw Hill/Irwin, 2004

[4] Hurd, Mark and Lars Nyberg, *The Value Factor, How Global Leaders Use Information for Growth and Competitive Advantage,* Bloomberg Press, 2004

[5] Collins, Jim, *Good to Great,* Harper Business, 2001

[6] Joyce, William and Nitin Nohria and Bruce Robertson, *What Really Works,* Harper Business, 2003

[7] Brown John Seely, and Estee Solomon Gray, "The People are the Company," *Fast Company,* Issue 1, November 1995

[8] Byrne, J. A. "The Horizontal Corporation." *Business Week,* December 20, 1993, pp. 76-81.

[9] Goleman, Daniel, and Richard Boyatzis and Annie McKee, *Primal Leadership: Realizing the Power of Emotional Intelligence,* Harvard Business School Press, 2002

[10] McCormack, Kevin, 'Business Process Orientation: Do You Have It?', *Quality Progress,* January 2001

[11] Ibid

[12] http://www.forbes.com/work/2005/03/08/cx_0308mckinsey.html

[13] Porter, Michael, 'What is Strategy?', *Harvard Business Review,* November-December 1996.

Appendix 1:

The Judicious Use of Reference Frameworks

Any firm interested in taking advantage of the available research on process frameworks may wish to investigate data from reference sources such as The MIT Process Handbook, The American Productivity & Quality Center (APQC), The Value Chain Group, and The Supply Chain Council.

These reference sources offer valuable insight on a number of topics, including, but not limited to, enterprise level frameworks, process classifications, process designs, process performance measures, and some insight on "best practices."

The data from these sources can be best used to stimulate idea generation or assist in diagnosis, as opposed to being used to prescribe what a given firm should do.

These reference sources rightly concentrate on the "what" of process. They represent processes in a static, linear view. It's important to remember that for your use, in the real world, what really counts is the cross-functional flow – not just what is done – but who does what.

How can you best use these reference sources? Outlined below is a brief treatment of some of the principal applications. For further details, readers are encouraged to visit the respective Web sites of The MIT Process Handbook, The American Productivity & Quality Center (APQC), The Value Chain Group, and The Supply Chain Council.

Developing an Enterprise Process View

Firms preparing to develop an enterprise level process view can take advantage of the high level MIT Business Activity Model

(BAM), the APQC's process classification framework (PCF), the Value Chain Group's value chain reference model (VCOR), and the Supply Chain Council's supply chain operations reference model (SCOR) to stimulate their leadership team's thinking on what type of schematic would best suit their own organization.

The work on the Process Handbook project began in 1991 at the MIT Center for Coordination Science. It has been reported to involve over forty university researchers, students, and various industrial sponsors. The effort of developing the business content for the MIT Process Handbook began to build momentum around 1995, and since 1996 the commercial application of the data has been licensed to an MIT spin-off company, called Phios Corporation (www.phios.com).[1]

The Process Handbook includes generic models of business activities, specific case examples, and frameworks for classifying knowledge around processes. The highest level model, called the MIT Business Activity Model (BAM), employs single word descriptions, as depicted in Figure A.1, for the five basic activities that occur in most businesses: Buy, Make, Sell, Design, and Manage.

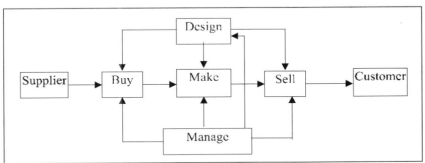

Figure A.1. The MIT Business Activity Model
(Source: http://ccs.mit.edu/ph/)

The longstanding reputation of MIT as an academic institution dedicated to advancing knowledge can be useful in bringing credibility to the task of educating leadership on the merits of the process view.

One of the most distinguishing features of the analysis in the MIT Process Handbook is that it employs a tool called the "process compass," which presents a two-dimensional view of process analysis. Unlike other reference models, it not only looks at the typical vertical view of breaking a process into its different parts, but it also has the second dimension of categorizing a process into its different types.[2]

Other models commonly look at the vertical view. For example, a large process like "Sell" can be decomposed into its smaller components such as Identify Prospects, Inform Potential Customers, Obtain an Order, Deliver Product or Service, etc. But the MIT Process Handbook goes beyond that and facilitates the horizontal view, which asks questions about specialization and generalization. For example, as it relates to a large process like "Sell," the specialization question considers aspects such as "Sell What" and "Sell How," and the generalization question considers where "Sell" fits into the even higher order of things, like "Exchange" and "Provide." This is potentially a very powerful feature to create a deeper understanding of the components of a given process.

APQC's PCF can also be useful in stimulating thinking in the development of an enterprise process model. The APQC was founded in 1977 and initially focused on its mission of increasing productivity in organizations. In 1992, The International Benchmarking Clearinghouse was launched and facilitated the APQC in becoming a primary repository for best practices and a valuable source of data on various topics, including process improvement.

On the APQC Web site, the data on process improvement resides in the section on "Benchmarking and Best Practices." Given its mission of productivity improvement, it stands to reason that the APQC would focus on process improvement as opposed to broad based process management. As stated on the Web site, the APQC position is "You must understand a process before you can improve it. To get a clear picture of a process, you have to determine what is being done, where it is being done, and how it is being done."[3]

The first version of the Process Classification Framework

(PCF) was developed in 1993, and the current 2005 version is depicted in table form below. The PCF was developed by APQC and member companies as an open standard to facilitate improvement through process management and benchmarking regardless of industry, size, or geography. The PCF organizes operating and management processes into 12 enterprise-level categories, including process groups and a large number of underlying processes and associated activities.

The 2005 Version of the APQC PCF
1. Develop Vision and Strategy
2. Design and Develop Products and Services
3. Market and Sell Products and Services
4. Deliver Products and Services
5. Manage Customer Service
6. Develop and Manage Human Capital
7. Manage Information Technology
8. Manage Financial Resources
9. Acquire, Construct, and Manage Property
10. Manage Environmental Health and Safety
11. Manage External Relationships
12. Manage Knowledge, Improvement, and Change
(Source: www.apqc.org)

The APQC PCF does not use single word descriptors for the high-level business processes and some observers have noted that the language in the PFC may reinforce a functional view. However, it does differentiate between Operating Processes (the first five cited) and Management and Support Processes. This can provide a useful perspective. Further, the reputation of the APQC and their work in identifying best practice companies such as Air Products can be useful in educating leaders on the merits of the process view. Also, the long list of resources on the process improvement section of the APQC Web site represents potentially useful information.

Supply chain centric companies will find the Supply Chain Council's SCOR model particularly appealing and thought provok-

ing in the development of a high level view of the business in process terms. The Air Products Enterprise Blueprint model depicted in
Chapter 3 is predicated on the simple language of the SCOR model.

The Supply-Chain Council (SCC) was organized in 1996, as an
independent, not-for-profit, global corporation with membership
open to all companies and organizations interested in applying and
advancing the state-of-the-art in supply-chain management systems
and practices.

The Supply Chain Operations Reference-model (SCOR) is a
product of the SCC. It captures the Council's consensus view of
supply chain management. The SCOR-model provides a comprehensive framework that links business process, metrics, best practices, and technology features into a cohesive structure to improve
the effectiveness of supply chain management and related supply
chain improvement activities.

According to the SCC scope statement, "The SCOR-model has
been developed to describe the business activities associated with all
phases of satisfying a customer's demand. The Model itself con-
tains several sections and is organized around the five primary management processes of Plan, Source, Make, Deliver, and Return. By
describing supply chains using these process building blocks, the
model can be used to describe supply chains that are very simple or
very complex using a common set of definitions." The elegant sim-
plicity of the SCOR model – Plan, Source, Make, Deliver, and Return – is one of its most distinguishing features.[4]

Schlegel and Smith reported that many companies already util-
ize the SCOR model to identify and prioritize process improvement
opportunities.[5] They noted in the March 2005 issue of *Supply Chain
Management Review* that companies that integrate SCOR, Lean, and
Six Sigma models see as much as ten times the continuous-
improvement benefits as those that undertake the programs indi-
vidually. Yet, they also contend that the SCOR model, by itself, may
not be enough, because it does not encompass processes such as
sales, marketing, and product development.[6]

The recent launch of the Value-Chain Operations Reference
Model (VCOR), which intends to describe the business activities

associated with all phases of satisfying customer needs, appears to support this perspective. The VCOR model proposes to include the business activities of partners, developers, marketers, suppliers, logistics, and point of sale and aftermarket service providers across the enterprise for both products and services.

In the September 20, 2005 edition of the *BPTrends Email Advisor*, Paul Harmon compared the merits of SCOR versus VCOR. Harmon outlined the merits of both SCOR and VCOR and provided background on the merits of creating an entire value chain Reference Model. He concluded that:

> The VCOR model provides a complete, internally consistent framework for modeling a complete value chain. The first draft of the VCOR model is complete, and the VCG has scheduled conference presentations and workshops for this fall. VCOR has comparable depth to SCOR and, like SCOR, includes a methodology, templates, measures, and best practices. Obviously, since the group that created VCOR is small and the framework is new, VCOR doesn't have the validated detail or the broad user base that SCOR has, but it will presumably acquire it as other companies learn about VCOR and join in the effort. More information on the VCG and the VCOR model is available at www.value-chain.org.[7]

Stimulating Thought on Measurement

The benefit of looking at these reference models is not limited to the insights from the macro blocks that the models depict, it also extends to the typical measures of performance listed in these reference sources for each of the macro blocks.

A company embarking on the improvement or redesign of a major cross-functional process can use these reference models at several points in the improvement effort; in the initial project definition, in detailed analysis and even in the design and implementation phases.

In the initial scoping or project definition phase of an improvement project, these reference sources can provide insight on a broad range of metrics that might be used in establishing baseline performance data. For many companies, especially those which are used to measuring predominately traditional financial metrics, the breadth of measurement options can be an eye-opener.

For example, if a firm is launching a project to improve the performance of the new product development process, there is considerable insight available from sources such as the APQC Web site in the full range of metrics related to time-based measures of product development performance. A sample of these time-based metrics is depicted in the Table below.

Time-based Metrics
▪ Cycle times by major development step
▪ Development time (actual to forecast)
▪ NPV, ROI, break-even time
▪ Time customer(s) involved in project
▪ Time for market testing
▪ Time from development to maturity
▪ Time from introduction to maturity
▪ Time to determine patentability
▪ Time to develop a product specification
▪ Time to make conceptual mock-ups
▪ Time to market
▪ Time to perform a business environment assessment
▪ Time to prepare a business plan
▪ Time to profitability
▪ Time to release engineering drawings
▪ Time to set up pilot production
▪ Time to verify design

Table A.2. Time-Based Metrics
(Source: www.apqc.org)

Alternatively, a firm contemplating the improvement of the "order fulfillment" or "order to cash" process may wish to examine the definition of a "perfect order" in the SCOR data and the related metrics. To illustrate, SCOR's definition of a "perfect order" is shown in Table A.3 below.

▪ A "perfect order" is defined as an order that meets all of the following standards:
▪ Delivered complete; all items on order are delivered in the quantities requested
▪ Delivered on time to customer's request date, using the customer's definition of on-time delivery
▪ Documentation supporting the order including packing slips, bills of lading, invoices, etc., is complete and accurate
▪ Perfect condition: Faultlessly installed (as applicable), correct configuration, customer-ready, no damage

Table A.3. Perfect Order Fulfillment Metrics
(Source: Supply Chain Council SCOR Model Version 7.0)

One caution for firms using these reference models is to be sensitive to the powerful role of language. The terms used for various activities in the available reference models do vary and may not reflect the language in common use within a firm. Accordingly, alignment of vocabulary and in some cases, targeted education on the meaning of terms is recommended.

Another caution pertains to the use of "best-practice" information available from several of these reference sources. Some of the "best practice" information may be several years old. In some cases, the data may refer to "past practice" as opposed to "best practice" and so caution should be exercised in the use of this information.

All in all, the reference models can serve to stimulate thinking and provide valuable sources of data for idea generation, model development, and general guidance. The challenge is to use the information judiciously to go beyond viewing processes in a static, linear view. Remember that for your use, in the real world, what really counts is the cross-functional flow of value creating activities – not just what is done – but who does what.

References.

[1] http://www.mitpress.mit.edu/books/chapters/0262134292chapm1.pdf

[2] Malone, W. Thomas, and Kevin Crowston, and George A. Herman, *Organizing Business Knowledge: The MIT Process Handbook,* The MIT Press, 2003

[3] http://www.apqc.org

[4] http://www.supply-chain.org/index.ww

[5] Schlegel, Gregory L., and Richard C. Smith, 'The Next Stage of Supply Chain Excellence', *Supply Chain Management Review*, March 1, 2005

[6] Ibid

[7] Harmon, Paul, 'The VCG and the SCC', BPTrends Email Advisor, Volume 3, Number 15, September 20, 2005

APPENDIX 2:

A Business Process Orientation Survey Instrument

Process View (PV)
1. The average employee views the business as a series of linked processes.
2. Process terms such as input, output, process, and process owners are used in conversation in the organization.
3. The business processes are sufficiently defined so that most people in the organization know how they work.

Process Jobs (PJ)
1. Jobs are usually multidimensional and not just simple tasks
2. Jobs include frequent problem solving.
3. People are constantly learning new things on the job.

Process Management and Measurement systems (PM)
1. Process performance is measured in your organization.
2. Process measurements are defined.
3. Resources are allocated based on process.
4. Specific process performance goals are in place.
5. Process outcomes are measured.

Interdepartmental Dynamics (ID)
Interdepartmental Conflict
1. Most departments in this business get along well with each other.
2. When members of several departments get together, tensions frequently run high.

3. People in one department generally dislike interacting with those from other departments.
4. Employees from different departments feel that the goals of their respective departments are in harmony with each other.
5. Protecting one's departmental turf is considered to be a way of life in this business unit.
6. The objectives pursued by the marketing department are incompatible with those of the manufacturing department.
7. There is little or no interdepartmental conflict in this business unit.

Interdepartmental Connectedness
1. In this business unit, it is easy to talk with virtually anyone you need to, regardless of rank or position.
2. There is ample opportunity for informal "hall talk" among individuals from different departments in this business unit.
3. In this business unit, employees from different departments feel comfortable calling each other when the need arises.
4. Managers here discourage employees from discussing work-related matters with those who are not their immediate superiors and subordinates.
5. People around here are quite accessible to those in other departments.
6. Communications from one department to another are expected to be routed through "proper channels."
7. Junior managers in my department can easily schedule meetings with junior managers in other departments.

Organizational Performance (OP)
Measures of Esprit de Corps
1. People in this business unit are genuinely concerned about the needs and problems of each other.
2. A team spirit pervades all ranks in this business unit.
3. Working for this business unit is like being part of a family.
4. People in this business unit feel emotionally attached to each other.

5. People in this business unit feel like they are "in it together."
6. This business unit lacks an "esprit de corps."
7. People in this business unit view themselves as independent individuals who have to tolerate others around them.

Overall Performance (5= excellent, 1= poor)

1. Please rate the overall performance of your business unit last year.
2. Please rate the overall performance of the business unit last year relative to major competitors.

Copyright©2002, DRK Research and Consulting LLC

For further details, go to: http://www.drkresearch.org/

Recommended Reading

Barwise, Patrick and Sean Meehan, *Simply Better: Winning and Keeping Customers by Delivering What Matters Most*, Harvard Business School Press, 2004.

Bensaou, M. and Michael Earl, "The Right Mind-Set for Managing Information Technology," *Harvard Business Review*, September-October 1998.

Abrahamson, Eric, *Change Without Pain*, Harvard Business School Press, 2004.

Brache, Alan, *How Organizations Work*, Wiley, 2002.

Bossidy, Larry and Ram Charan, *Execution: The Discipline of Getting Things Done*, Crown Business, 2002.

Christensen, Clayton M., and Scott D. Anthony and Erik A. Roth, *Seeing What's Next*, Harvard Business School Press, 2004.

Collins, Jim, *Good to Great*, Harper Business, 2001.

Cooper, Robert G., *Winning at New Products: Accelerating the Process from Idea to Launch*, Perseus Books, 1993.

Davenport, Thomas H., *Process Innovation*, Harvard Business School Press, 1993.

Davenport, Thomas H., "Putting the Enterprise into the Enterprise System," *Harvard Business Review*, July - August 1998.

Drucker, Peter, *Management Challenges of the 21st Century*, Harper Business, 1999.

Feld, Charlie S., and Donna B. Stoddard, "Getting IT Right," *Harvard Business Review*, February 2004.

Fingar, Peter, *Extreme Competition: Innovation and the Great 21st Century Business Reformation,* Meghan-Kiffer Press, 2006.

Fingar, Peter, and Joseph Bellini, *The Real-Time Enterprise,* Meghan-Kiffer Press, 2004.

Galbraith, Jay, *Designing Organizations*, Jossey-Bass, 1995.

Galbraith, Jay R., *Designing the Customer-Centric Organization: A Guide to Strategy, Structure, and Process*, Wiley 2005.

Goleman, Daniel, and Richard Boyatzis and Annie McKee, *Primal Leadership: Realizing the Power of Emotional Intelligence*, Harvard Business School Press, 2002.

Hagel III, John and John Seely Brown, "Your Next IT Strategy," *Harvard Business Review*, October 2001.

Hamel, Gary, *Leading the Revolution*, Harvard Business School Press, 2000.

Hamel, Gary, "Strategy as Revolution," *Harvard Business Review*, July-August 1996.

Hammer, Michael, "Process Management and the Future of Six Sigma," *Sloan Management Review*, Winter 2002.

Hammer, Michael, "The Superefficient Company," *Harvard Business Review*, September 2001.

Hammer, Michael and Steven Stanton, "How Process Enterprises Really Work," *Harvard Business Review*, November - December 1999.

Hammer, Michael, *The Agenda*, Crown Business, 2001.

Harmon, Paul, *Business Process Change*, Morgan Kaufmann, 2003

Herbold, Robert J., *The Fiefdom Syndrome*, Doubleday, 2004

Joyce, William and Nitin Nohria and Bruce Robertson, *What Really Works*, Harper Business, 2003.

Kaplan, Robert S. and David P. Norton, *The Balanced Scorecard*, Harvard Business School Press, 1996

Kaplan, Robert S. and David P. Norton, "Having Trouble with Your Strategy? Then Map It," *Harvard Business Review*, September-October 2000.

Kaplan, Robert S. and David P. Norton, *The Strategy-Focused Organization*, Harvard Business School Press, 2001.

Kaplan, Robert S. and David P. Norton, "Using the Balanced Scorecard as a Strategic Management System," *Harvard Business Review*, January- February 1996.

Kotter, John, "What Leaders Really Do," *Harvard Business Review*, Special Issue December 2001.

Kotter, John, "Leading Change: Why Transformation Efforts Fail," *Harvard Business Review*. March-April 1995.

Majchrak, Ann and Qianwei Wang, "Breaking the Functional Mindset in Process Organizations," *Harvard Business Review*, September - October 1996, pgs 92-99.

McCormack, Kevin P., and William C. Johnson with William T. Walker, Supply Chain Networks and Business Process Orientation; Advanced Strategies and Best Practices, CRC Press, 2000.

Porter, Michael, "What is Strategy?" *Harvard Business Review*, November-December 1996.

Porter, Michael, "Strategy and the Internet," *Harvard Business Review*, March 2001.

Rodin, Robert, *Free, Perfect, and Now*, Simon & Schuster, 1999.

Ross, Jeanne W. and Peter Weill, "Six IT Decisions Your IT People Shouldn't Make," *Harvard Business Review*, November 2002.

Rummler, Geary A. and Alan Brache, *Improving Performance: How to Manage the White Space on the Organization Chart*, Jossey-Bass, 1995.

Smith, Dick and Jerry Blakeslee with Richard Koonce, *Strategic Six Sigma; Best Practices from the Executive Suite*, Wiley, 2002.

Smith, Howard and Peter Fingar, *Business Process Management: The Third Wave*, Meghan-Kiffer Press, 2003.

Smith, Howard and Peter Fingar, *IT Doesn't Matter: Business Processes Do*, Meghan-Kiffer Press, 2004.

Treacy, Michael and Fred Wiersema, *The Discipline of Market Leaders*, Addison Wesley, 1995.

Treacy, Michael, *Double-Digit Growth*, Portfolio, 2003.

Index

About the Author

ANDREW SPANYI is internationally recognized for his work on Business Process Management. He has over three decades of management and consulting practice experience. He has managed or consulted on over 130 major improvement projects and has participated in the development and delivery of dozens of sales and management training programs.

Andrew's areas of practice leadership include Business Process Improvement and Management, Strategy Clarification, Performance Measurement, and Change Management.

He has delivered keynote speeches at conferences in North America and Europe and has published articles with a broad cross-section of print and e-magazines. He is a member of the research team at the Babson Process Management Research Center, the chair of the education committee for The Association of Business Process Management Professionals, and an editorial board member with the BPM Institute.

He is the author of *Business Process Management is a Team Sport: Play It to Win!*

Contact Andrew Spanyi at andrew@spanyi.com.

EXTREME COMPETITION

INNOVATION AND THE GREAT 21ST CENTURY BUSINESS REFORMATION

PETER FINGAR

The definitive guide to total global competition.
www.mkpress.com/extreme

Watch for forthcoming titles.

MK

Meghan-Kiffer Press

Tampa, Florida, USA

www.mkpress.com

Innovation at the Intersection of Business and Technology